T0162681

HEAR *the* WORD

Listening to the Eternal Word
in the Contemporary World

Dr. JAMES A. PRETTE

iUniverse, Inc.
Bloomington

iUniverse books may be ordered through booksellers or by contacting:

iUniverse
1663 Liberty Drive
Bloomington, IN 47403
www.iuniverse.com
1-800-Authors (1-800-288-4677)

ISBN: 978-1-4620-1374-6 (sc)
ISBN: 978-1-4620-1376-0 (hc)
ISBN: 978-1-4620-1375-3 (ebook)

Printed in the United States of America

iUniverse rev. date: 04/22/2011

Table of Contents

Introduction

How is the spiritual formation of God's people happening?

One Sunday, I was in a youth-oriented church service where cheers greeted the announcement that there would be no sermon that night. The members of the congregation seemed pleased to have no sermon during the evening because, as one young man later told me, "Sermons wreck the flow of the night." Many of the church attendees apparently see sermons (and the instructive reading of biblical texts during a worship service) as interruptions to an authentic "experience of God's presence." Meanwhile, the congregation leapt to their feet to engage in loud postmodern choruses, some of which contained messages of questionable theological content.

At best, some of the postmodern Christians at this church dutifully accept sermons as an important part of the worship service, while they engage most enthusiastically with (what they believe to be) God through the worship music. Many describe sermons and worship singing as two distinct (and even conflicting) entities. When the above-mentioned service does have sermons, they are given in the contemporary language, history, and culture of the audience, but they often lack any real depth of exegetical respect for the actual texts of Scripture.

I have been a full-time evangelist through Young Life of Canada for over twenty years; for more than a decade, I have also been working as a teaching pastor with a church plant called The Place. This is an alternative congregation of Lambrick Park Church in Victoria, British Columbia, attracting over three hundred college-aged young people to a weekly Sunday night service. This is most remarkable for a Canadian church.[1] The purpose of Young Life is to proclaim the basic Gospel message to unchurched teenagers in their contemporary language, history, and culture. The purpose of The Place is to be a church. The Church is an ancient institution which, like the community of Israel before it, is the community of God's people that gathers weekly to listen to the Word of God read, sung, prayed, and preached for corporate and individual Spiritual formation.[2]

Many teenagers have been introduced to Christ through the Young Life ministry and have subsequently joined The Place as their church and as a place to grow in Christ. There is a difference between evangelism to those without any church involvement and the formative nurturing of Christians within churches. Some descriptions of what churches are doing (or are being encouraged to do) in our contemporary context are more akin to Young Life evangelism than a church. If emerging churches in the West are merely missional outreach vehicles, then where and how will the lifelong Spiritual formation of God's people happen?

Who is right?

After visiting a church service with two church colleagues, we were asked by our hosts to evaluate the sermon. One colleague (an American pastor) said that it was "excellent" because the preacher spoke with such passion. The other colleague (an African pastor) rated the sermon only "fair" because, though it spoke in the language, history, and culture of the group present, it would not speak to his own context. I rated the sermon as "poor" because there were far

---

1   The 2001 Canadian Religious Census indicates that the population of those attending traditional churches in Canada is a rapidly aging one. With a median age of 37.3 in Canada, the median age of Protestants is 41.9, while the median age of those with "no religion" is 31.1. Of those who claim to have "no religion," 74.3 percent are under forty-five, compared to 25.7 percent of Canadians over forty-five who claim to have "no religion." This has also been attested to by the research of Canadian sociologist Reginald Bibby in his book Fragmented Gods: The Poverty and Potential of Religion in Canada (Toronto, ON: Irwin, 1987).

2   See Chapter 2.

too many exegetical flaws in the interpretation of the biblical text that was preached from. Which one of us was right? We could all agree that the preacher was passionate, but the crucial question is whether the people were actually exposed to God's revelatory and formative Word that day. These are the questions that have driven me to pursue this exploration of authentic Christian preaching (the task I have before me) in this postmodern culture (the setting I find myself in).

The Three Parts of Persuasive Speech

In Chapter 1, I will explore the tri-focus of communication involving the content of the message, the context of the message, and the conveyor of the message. In *On Rhetoric*, Aristotle argued that there are three parts to persuasive speech: *pathos, ethos, and logos*.[3] These terms can be borrowed to distinguish three unique and essential parts of effective Christian proclamation. Each of these parts of persuasive speech is essential to authentic communication. I will argue that if one of these parts of a sermon is ignored, no real hearing of the Word occurs, and therefore, no real Christian formation takes place. This paradigm can also be used to evaluate any sermon to determine its effectiveness as a true communication of the authentic *logos* of the Word of God in the authentic *ethos* of the hearing audience, with the authentic *pathos* of Church leaders.

Chapter 2 is a theological reflection. Here I will explore and define a biblical theological paradigm for Spiritual[4] formation through biblical exposition that crosses cultural and generational boundaries. The *logos* of Christian Spiritual formation will be defined as the texts of the Christian Holy Scripture, exegeted and heard. I will argue that this has always been the vital work of the leaders of God's faith community in every generation.

---

3   See George A. Kennedy, On Rhetoric (New York, NY: Oxford University Press, 1991). Also, see Chapter 3.
4   I will always capitalize the word "Spirit," even in its adjectival form, when I am referring to the Holy Spirit of God, who is a person, and to that which belongs to Him.

Chapter 3 will discuss the cultural shift that has taken place in the *ethos* of Western culture, from a modernist worldview to a postmodern one, and its impact on Christian ministry, especially preaching. I will also discuss the essential nature of this *ethos*, especially focusing on the emergent church in the West, and the attitude toward preaching of several of its representative leaders.

In Chapter 4, I will describe the results of an exploratory study project investigating the *pathos* of a representative group of ten young emergent church conveyors and how they understand and practice the function of Spiritual formation within the context of their postmodern congregations. There is little consideration of the theological and sociological frameworks of the contemporary, postmodern, Western context of the emerging Church. There is also a lack of any articulation of a serious approach to Christian preaching that is at once authentically Christian (adhering to a biblical, historical Christian understanding of the function of the public hearing of God's Word) and, at the same time, authentically postmodern (truly engaging the language, culture, and history of the contemporary, postmodern, Western context).

Chapter 5 will put it all together with nine recommendations for contemporary Western conveyors of the authentic content of God's Word in the language, culture, and history of their actual hearer's context. These nine recommendations will literally spell out what *Christian* preaching will look like in this postmodern context.

Chapter 1
Communicating Spiritual Formation

The Communication and Contextualization Frameworks

Lesslie Newbigin returned home to England after serving as an Anglican missionary bishop in India. In his book *Foolishness to the Greeks*, he laments the fact that the Church has fallen into one of two traps as it has sought to engage its surrounding culture. The Church has either fallen into "indigenization," wherein the language, history, and culture of the surrounding *ethos* is compromised for the sake of preserving the peculiar culture of the Church, or into "adaptation," wherein the peculiar message of the Church is compromised for the sake of relating to the contemporary *ethos* of the particular culture.

> The weakness of the former was that it tended to relate the Christian message to the traditional cultural forms—forms that belonged to the past and from which young people were turning away under the pervasive influence of "modernization." The effect was to identify the gospel with the conservative elements in society. The weakness of the latter term, *adaptation*, was that it implied that what the missionary brought with him was the pure gospel, which had to be adapted to the receptor culture. It tended to obscure the fact that the gospel as embodied in the missionary's

preaching and practice was already an adapted gospel, shaped by his or her own culture.[5]

Newbigin advocates the use of the term "contextualization" to help us understand the "culture of the moment,"[6] differentiating between the message of the Gospel, the context of the culture of the Christian missionary, and the context of his contemporary cultural environment. Bruce J. Nicholls describes contextualization as "the translation of the unchanging content of the gospel of the kingdom into verbal form meaningful to the peoples in their separate cultures and within their particular existential situations."[7]

In this chapter we will examine the issues of effective communication in relation to Spiritual formation through biblical exposition. This will involve an application of communication theory to the discipline of preaching and an exploration of contextualization as a means to best translate the meaning of God's Word to each cultural context. An adaptation of Aristotle's three parts of persuasive speech (*logos, ethos,* and *pathos*)[8] can be used to examine the effectiveness of the preaching act. The authentic *logos* (the content of God's Word)[9] must be given in the authentic *ethos* (the perceived ability of the conveyor of the *logos* to connect with the receptor language, history, and culture of the contemporary context) with authentic *pathos* (the perceived authenticity, authority, and integrity of the conveyor of the message).[10]

Authentic Christian Spiritual formation has always connected the *logos* of God to the *ethos* of the contemporary audience

5   Lesslie Newbigin, Foolishness to the Greeks (Grand Rapids, MI: William B. Eerdmans Publishing Company, 1997), 2.

6   Ibid, 2.

7   Bruce J. Nicholls, "Theological Education and Evangelization," in J. D. Douglas (ed.), Let the Earth Hear His Voice (Minneapolis, MN: World Wide, 1975), 647.

8   George A. Kennedy, On Rhetoric (New York, NY: Oxford University Press, 1991).

9   The argument of Chapter 2 is that the authentic logos of Christian preaching will always be the exposing of the meaning of the texts of God's Holy Word, the Bible.

10   According to Descartes, "we may define them [passions] generally as the perceptions, feelings or emotions of the soul which we relate specially to it and which are caused, maintained and fortified by some movement of the spirits" in Passions of the Soul, 1, 2, quoted by Copleston, A History of Philosophy, vol. 4, 143.

through authentic *pathos*. With Newbigin's warnings, one can evaluate whether a specific Christian proclaimer has committed "indigenization," wherein the *ethos* is compromised for the sake of *logos*, or "adaptation," wherein the *logos* is compromised for the sake of *ethos*. Rather, one must "contextualize"[11] the unchanging *logos* to the contemporary *ethos* and speak with authentic *pathos*.

Newbigin also warns against the absorption of the *logos* into the *ethos* of the conveyor of the message. One must observe the "culture of the moment," differentiating between the cultural context of Spiritual formation and the context of the audience's cultural environment.[12] One must evaluate all three dimensions of authentic communication in the act of Christian Spiritual formation in the experience of a sermon. Figure 1 shows a scale of how one might evaluate the *logos* of the message being preached. One can appraise whether a sermon reaches a low, medium, or high standard in the exposing of the actual meaning of the text being exposed.

Evaluating the Logos

figure 1

low	med	high

LOGOS

The *logos* of the message can be evaluated on whether the messenger has correctly exegeted the text. This involves interpreting the message of the passage in its original contexts. These include its historical, cultural, and literary contexts.[13] The text of the *logos* was written to

---

11   See David J. Hesselgrave and Edward Rommen, Contextualization: Meanings, Methods and Models (Grand Rapids, MI: Baker Book House, 1989).

12   Lesslie Newbigin, Foolishness to the Greeks, 2.

13   Gordon Fee and Douglas Stewart, How to Read the Bible For All its Worth (Grand Rapids, MI: Zondervan, 1982).

a particular *ethos* at a particular time for a particular purpose. These contexts must be understood before one can apply the meaning of the text for the contemporary *ethos*. The message cannot mean what it never meant.[14] One danger is to take the text of Scripture and apply it directly to one's contemporary *ethos*, as in figure 2.

figure 2

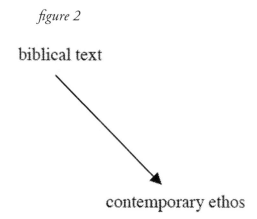

biblical text

biblical ethos   contemporary ethos

This accounts for many awkward applications of texts, written for culturally sensitive occasions, being applied inappropriately in contemporary settings, such as requiring women to cover their heads in churches. Brian Hebblethwaite warns,

> It is not even possible for us to mean what the writers of the Bible and the creeds meant just by saying what they said. We have to embark on the process of interpretation, in the light of our recognition both of their presuppositions and of our own, and struggle to express the truth of God and of God's acts for our own time.[15]

An equally dangerous approach is when a preacher begins with his own contemporary *ethos* and approaches the biblical text, looking

---

14   Dick Lucas, Proclamation Trust, 2000.
15   Brian Hebblethwaite, The Incarnation: Collected Essays in Christology (Cambridge, UK: University of Cambridge Press, 1987), 103.

for material he can take out of context to have the Bible say what he thinks his *ethos* needs to hear, as in figure 3. *The Big Idea of Biblical Preaching*[16] is a helpful book for applying Haddon Robinson's excellent concept of finding the one big idea in the biblical text passage and exposing it to the listeners through preaching. But the preacher must be most careful that his "one big idea" is not in fact his own "one small idea" eisogeted into the text, nor his own rendering of God's dynamic presence reduced to a mere moral principle or a feel-good, pop-psychology nuance.

figure 3

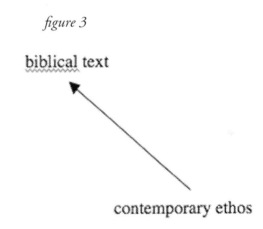

biblical text

biblical ethos   contemporary ethos

Rather, what one must do is to listen to the biblical text (the *logos*) and interpret what its message was to the original audience (biblical *ethos*) in light of its original context. Then one must take that message and contextualize it for one's own audience (contemporary *ethos*), as in figure 4.

---

16   Keith Willhite and Scott M. Gibson (eds.), The Big Idea of Biblical Preaching: Connecting the Bible to People (Grand Rapids, MI: Baker Books, 1998).

figure 4

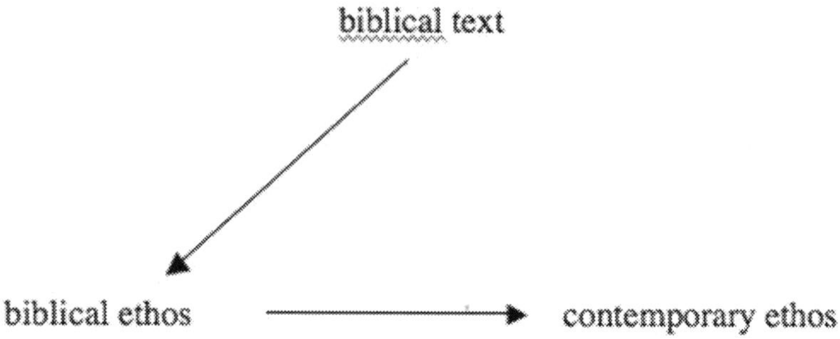

biblical text

biblical ethos ⟶ contemporary ethos

Os Guinness observes, "The only thing that is always relevant is the gospel."[17] Meanwhile, Chad Myers is right to warn against "reducing [the Scriptures] to morality tales for private spirituality."[18] He also writes, "Fortunately, post-modernism has exposed the fallacy of claims to either doctrinal or historic-critical objectivity."[19] He hopefully does not mean what others have taken to mean that there is no such thing as "objective truth." He hopefully means that the claim that one can reach a perfect, objective understanding of any text is a fallacy. God is objectively true. He reveals himself through his *logos*, the Word. This revelation comes to us as truth. It is objectively true, but received subjectively. The preacher's task is to listen, dig, mark, learn, meditate, argue, study, memorize, obey, and then proclaim, as best he can, what it meant and what it means.

Christian preachers must be especially careful when exegeting narrative. These parts of Scripture are given to us as "stories," but they are also the historic records of God's revealed salvation history events, his real historic work in the real world, not just the experience of how these stories make us feel. These are not private oracles through which individuals are meant to have their own personal religious experience. These are the corporate "stories" of the Spiritual formation of the authentic historic faith community that worships

---

17   http://www.christianitytoday.com/ct/2003/134/22.0.html
18   Ched Myers, Reading the Bible in the New Millennium (Sojourners Online Magazine, http://www.faithandvalues.com/tx/00/00/03/30/3044/index.html).
19   Ibid.

the God who has revealed himself in and through his personally breathed-out Word. As Peter Adam writes, "Christian gospel ministry involves explaining, preaching, applying and interpreting this sufficient Word so that people may be converted and congregations may be built up in faith, godliness and usefulness."[20]

Another contemporary compromise with postmodern culture is the rejection of expository preaching for greater spiritualist experientialism. Some have tried to link exegetically-based "expository preaching" with modernist intellectualism, in contrast with more "Spirit-led," spontaneous, postmodern, topical messages. John Woodhouse makes a convincing argument for the absurdity of this, stressing that the reasonable and clearly exegeted text and the Spirit are inseparable.[21] He rejects the attempt to bring a "balance" between these two extremes as heretical. He demonstrates that the illumination of the text of God's Word is the primary work and message of the Holy Spirit. He then calls for an embracing of the authentically Christian approach to interpreting and proclaiming the Word, which involves the dynamic synergy between the Spirit of God speaking and working through the Word of God read, exegeted, and taught.

Evaluating the Ethos

The evaluation of the *logos* of Spiritual formation through the preached message is only the first of the three parts of the communication of the eternal Word to one's contemporary audience. One can rank the *logos* of a message in one of three places: low, medium, or high. When one adds a second dimension of persuasive speech, one now has nine options in evaluating the preached message, as in figure 5. The *ethos* of the message is the perceived authenticity of the speaker, based on his ability to communicate in the language, culture, and

---

20   Peter Adam, "The Preacher and the Sufficient Word" in When God's Voice is Heard (Leicester, UK: Inter-Varsity Press, 1995), 29.
21   John Woodhouse, "The Preacher and the Living Word" in When God's Voice is Heard (Leicester, UK: Inter-Varsity Press, 1995), 44–46.

history of his audience. One cannot only evaluate how well the preacher exposes the authentic *logos*, but also how well the preacher reaches the authentic *ethos* of the receptor language of his audience. One may have the very Word of God to convey, but if one is not perceived as authentic, the message is not heard.

figure 5

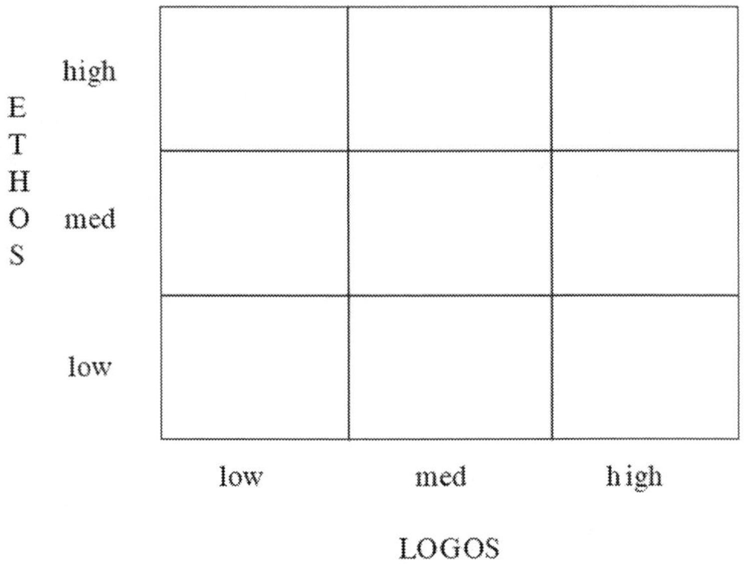

In this case, "*ethos*" is not used strictly in the sense of Aristotle's *Rhetoric*. By "*ethos*," Aristotle means something more akin to the English word "*ethic*."[22] The credibility of the speaker is judged on his perceived character. There it is used to mean the credibility of the conveyor of the message, but here "*ethos*" will be used more in the sense of his ability to connect with the "*ethnicity*" of the audience—their language, history, and culture.

22   Andre Resner Jr., Preacher and Cross: Person and Message in Theology and Rhetoric (Grand Rapids, MI: William B. Eerdmans Publishing Company, 1999), 20. Also, see Jong Sung Rhee, A New Anthropology from the Perspective of Theology in Theology in the Service of the Church: Essays in Honor of Thomas W. Gillespie (Grand Rapids, MI: William B. Eerdmans Publishing Company, 2000), 168–170.

George Barna's *Generation Next*[23] is an insightful expose of the twenty-something generation in America, and it describes how Christian ministries can reach out to this unique group. The most helpful section for applying understanding of the contemporary Western *ethos* is found in the ninth chapter, entitled "New Rules, New Challenges." These fifteen "rules" are 1) Personal Relationships count, institutions don't; 2) The process is more important than the product; 3) We must aggressively pursue diversity among people; 4) Enjoying people and life is more important than productivity, profitability, or achievement; 5) Change is good; 6) The development of character is more crucial than achievement; 7) You can't always count on your family to be there for you, but it is your best hope for emotional support; 8) Each individual must assume responsibility for his or her own world; 9) Whenever necessary, gain control—and use it wisely; 10) Don't waste time searching for absolutes. There are none; 11) One person can make a difference in the world—but not much; 12) Life is hard and then you die, but because it's the only life we've got, we may as well endure it, enhance it, and enjoy it as best we can; 13) Spiritual truth may take many forms; 14) Express your rage; and 15) Technology is our natural ally. We may not agree with these statements, but we must understand them to best communicate in the history and culture of the receptor language.

Emergent leader Dan Kimball offers ways of connecting the Christian life with contemporary postmoderns in his book *The Emerging Church.*[24] He provides helpful charts, photos, thoughts, and suggestions on ways to engage the postmodern *ethos*. In preaching, he argues for an exegetically-based topical approach, saying,

> I use a mix of both expository and topical preaching, a type of preaching I call "theotopical." We should be expository in terms of doing the right exegetical work for biblically rooted messages. But at the same time preaching is an opportunity to shape a

---

23   George Barna, Generation Next: What You Need to Know About Today's Youth (Ventura, CA: Regal Books, 1995).
24   Dan Kimball, The Emerging Church: Vintage Christianity for New Generations (Grand Rapids, MI: Zondervan, 2003).

theological worldview for people by telling the story. Every time I preach I clearly know what theological concept I am trying to teach and how it fits into the story of the Bible.[25]

In his book *The Unknown God*,[26]Alister McGrath examines how the Christian Church can communicate the Gospel to this postmodern culture. His argument is that one must discover the common ground from which to start the proclamation of the Gospel and then couch it in the terms and interests of the hearers. This is precisely what the Apostle Paul does in Athens on Mars Hill in Acts 17, where McGrath takes his title.

McGrath demonstrates how one can see that there is a common Spiritual hunger in every person, and he uses this archetypal longing to begin his exploration of the claims of the Christian faith. He uses Plato's classical Greek metaphor of "The Cave" and postmodern sentiment to build a case for a hearing of the Christian worldview and the particulars of the historic biblical message. The book includes many pictures and has a colorful, sparse layout that is inviting and readable for this, our Western *ethos*. This book is helpful as training material for Christians to be fitted for sensitivity to the basic searching needs of the postmodern *ethos*. Walter Brueggemann argues for contemporary preachers to become poets who "speak against a prose filled world."[27] He sees this as the way postmodern Christian proclaimers can subversively undermine the misunderstandings of their generation with evocative words that generate new vitality in this flat reductionist culture.

With *Reckless Hope*,[28] Todd Hahn and David Verhaagen have produced a helpful analysis of how the Church can reach the "Buster" generation of today with the authentic revealed Gospel of yesterday. They demonstrate how this next generation is unique from

---

25   Kimball, 188.

26   Alister McGrath, The Unknown God (Grand Rapids, MI: Zondervan, 1999).

27   Walter Brueggemann, Finally Comes the Poet (Minneapolis, MN: Fortress Press, 1989), 3.

28   Todd Hahn and David Verhaagen, Reckless Hope (Grand Rapids, MI: Baker Books, 1996).

the "Boomers" who went before them and who fill our evangelical churches today. They break their analysis into three parts, offering 1) A description of the "Buster" generation, 2) A prescription for offering them the revealed message of "Hope," and 3) The implications involved in developing this approach to meeting "Busters" with the authentic Christian Gospel.

Hahn and Verhaagen do an excellent job of describing the *ethos* of this generation, drawing on some statistical research as well as some anecdotal evidence. They faithfully adhere to a desire to present the authentic Christian Gospel found only in the Scriptures. They also make helpful and wise suggestions when challenging the local church to put this into practice. Their three-angled paradigm for presenting the Gospel today is very helpful; creation, covenant, and community can communicate the message and connect with the interests of "Busters."

They also provide an excellent discussion of the dangers of the modernist approach to the Bible that treats God's revelation as merely a "road map" or an encyclopedia of morality (chapter three). The authors also make a good case for the preservation of the authentic "old story" of grace and truth found only in the Scriptures (chapter seven). They claim—correctly—that one of the great barriers to the heroic life of authentic Christianity is biblical illiteracy. These are helpful and provocative statements. Unfortunately, the authors do not go far enough in describing the authentic locus of Christian Spiritual formation being under the authority of the Holy Scriptures. What does it look like to not treat the Bible as a road map of morality or to proclaim the old story or to correct biblical illiteracy? The missing element is a description of authentic Christian proclamation of the revelation of God. There is good material here on communicating the Gospel. It is helpful to articulate the overarching themes of God's old story in new language, such as creation, covenant, and community. The uniqueness of each new generation must be understood. Yet there is not a clear picture of the authentic activity of the Christian, who is primarily one who listens to God's Word. How can the Christian person live into the text through regular reading, hearing, studying, meditating (mumbling), and memorizing, and how can the text (and the very Spirit of God) live into the Christian person? It must be stressed that whatever the character of the generation, the authentic activity of the Christian in that culture is to be the "salt" (preserver of the Word, law, and Gospel) and the "light" (the proclaimer of the revealed Word, law, and Gospel). It ought to be primarily through regular Lord's Day worship that the Christian becomes equipped to be a hearer and doer of God's Word.

With *Homiletic*,[29] David Buttrick has written a massive tome on preaching. The volume is entirely devoted to his argument for a preaching style he calls "moves." "Moves" are a structured way of thinking and speaking, taking one's ideas and sermons through loops of argument beginning with statements, moving to counter statements, then to development of the idea, and finally to a conclusion of the thought. He argues that this is the natural way of thinking and speaking in the postmodern setting. It is, therefore, the best way to structure a sermon. It is a way of connecting with the *ethos* of this generation.

This is a helpful work for the postmodern preacher. Buttrick takes the *ethos* of his audience seriously and the *logos* of the Word of God seriously. Putting these two elements (audience and message) together is the task of the authentic Christian proclaimer. The committed proclaimer of God's Word in the postmodern setting will need to understand these two elements intimately.

Evaluating the Pathos

The evaluation of the *logos* and the *ethos* of the preached message are only two of the three parts of the communication of the eternal Word to one's contemporary audience. One can rank the *logos* and the *ethos* of a message in a grid of nine options. Finally, one must also evaluate the perceived *pathos* of the message. This adds a third dimension to the evaluation process, enabling anyone to assign the sermon to one of twenty-seven options, as in figure 6.

---

29   David Buttrick, Homiletic (Philadelphia, PA: Fortress Press, 1987).

figure 6

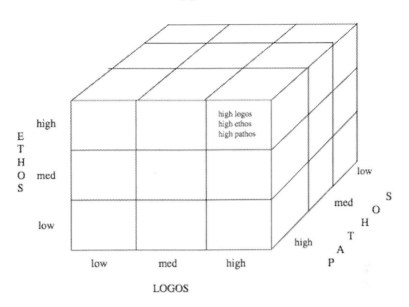

The *pathos* of a message is the ability of the speaker to connect with his audience. It is the perceived authenticity of the speaker. What allows an audience to receive a message depends on the perception of the speaker as one worth listening to, one who can hold the audience's attention. The *pathos* of Christian Spiritual formation is the authentic Spirit-formed conveyor of God's *logos* in the contemporary *ethos*. The goal is to be in the one quadrant that would have the message be the authentic *logos* in the authentic *ethos* with authentic *pathos*.

Here then is a tool to evaluate the full measure of a given message. After hearing a message, my wife, Liz, and I will ask each other, "So, how was the message: *logos*, *ethos*, and *pathos*?" Then we will rate it as high, medium, or low on each dimension. The serious conveyor of God's Word must aim for the only acceptable square out of the twenty-seven possibilities. Only that would be the proclamation of God's authentic Word to the authentic contemporary audience by an authentically reliable proclaimer. And, only that will lead to the kind of authentic Spiritual formation in the lives of the hearers we want from preaching.

Philip Yancey is a master at articulating the angst of believing in the God revealed to us in the Scriptures, while looking at the existential realities of the life of faith with eyes wide open. Sometimes it is difficult to reconcile the promises of the life of faith with the daily realities of the normal Christian life experience. In his book *Reaching for the Invisible God*,[30] Yancey devotes his best inquisitive prose to the issue of doubt. He uses his own life history to explore the little bit that he argues one can confidently say that one can tacitly "know." He then begins to systematically build back up what he argues is the basics of what one can also "know" through rational demonstration and observation. This is the kind of *pathos* that engages the postmodern Western person.

Darrell Johnson comments,

> The younger generation, in preaching, is looking for authenticity in the communicator; the communicator having something to say that they don't hear anywhere else, and the communicator treating young people as smart and not dumbing it down and buying into the television view of a young person. I think [being] given the chance to enter into a text and engage that text is what young people are looking for, and is much more powerful than the "pabulum" that they are given. And I think young people would flock to a church where, either young or old, a communicator was to do that.[31]

---

30   Philip Yancey, Reaching for the Invisible God (Grand Rapids, MI: Zondervan, 2000).

31   Darrell Johnson, panel discussion on the teachings of Brian McLaren at Regent College, Vancouver, BC, Feb. 2005.

The Art of Christian Persuasion

Em Griffin was once on the staff of Young Life USA. In *The Mind Changers*,[32] he brings the skills learned from years of "earning the right to be heard" by hundreds of uninterested, cynical, pagan American teenagers to the task of proclaiming the good news of Christ. Using humor, Griffin offers Christian apologists some great points to consider in "the art of Christian persuasion." This subtitle to the book is the sentiment of his whole approach. One cannot force anyone to believe anything, whether through clever argument or violence. The best one can do is learn the art of loving people and the art of loving the message of Jesus Christ and bring those two loves together in introducing friends to the friendly God. This is perceived as authentic *pathos* in this generation.

A helpful picture of Spiritual formation that Griffin uses throughout the book is that of candle making. In candle making, one takes the wax through the stages of becoming a candle. One must melt the wax, mold it, and wait for it to harden. Here are the steps to the art of authentic Spiritual formation, especially in the postmodern context. One must melt the hearts of those one wishes to reach through building trust-filled relationships of love and friendship. Next, one must mold the ideas of the pre-Christian through gentle persuasion, transparent modeling of the normal Christian life, and clear presentation of the historic biblical message. Finally, one must harden (solidify) the commitment to the new life in Christ through an ongoing discipleship relationship with the pre- and new believer. This is a very helpful book for all believers to use to grow in confidence and interest in communicating and demonstrating the good news of the Christian hope.

---

32   Em Griffen, The Mind Changers (Wheaton, IL: Tyndale House Publishers, 1976).

Dumbing Down the Story

Ralph and Gregg Lewis have presented a helpful volume called *Inductive Preaching,*[33] which emphasizes the need for good storytelling in postmodern preaching. They make an excellent case for the fact that this is the essential means of faithful biblical preaching. They stress the fact that the Scriptures come to us primarily as narrative and are, therefore, story. The Bible is basically one long story—God's story. This is his revelation of himself through his own story about himself and his personal revelation through the lives and histories of his people. The art of good storytelling is an essential skill one must master to strike authentic *pathos* as a proclaimer of God's Word. Jesus primarily asked questions and told stories. The Church today tends to give answers and lectures. In this postmodern culture, there is especially a vital need for the skills of good storytelling.

One of the sensitive issues in this contemporary climate is the popular rebellion against any kind of institutional authority. If one is perceived to be a paternalistic, archaic, hierarchical, bigoted Church spokesperson, spouting dead theoretical rhetoric, one will have a small audience of postmodern listeners. But if one tells a story with real contemporary *pathos*, one will be perceived as being captivating, real, and relevant. Then one will find a waiting audience who will listen, be fed, and come to hear the truth of God's Word.

There are some ways that one must resist a compromise with a kind of *pathos* that is not biblical. Marva Dawn brings her witty and insightful mind to bear on the controversial issue of worship in today's churches in her book *A Royal "Waste" of Time.*[34] She speaks from a liturgical framework and bias, but she makes a very good case for the value and necessity of historic, traditional liturgy in Christian Spiritual formation. In this postmodern setting, there is a growing interest in tradition, mystery, and sacred space. There has been a growing distrust and distaste for the sometimes antiseptic,

---

33   Ralph Lewis and Gregg Lewis, Inductive Preaching (Wheaton, IL: Crossway Books, 1983).
34   Marva J. Dawn, A Royal "Waste" of Time: The Splendor of Worshiping God and Being Church for the World (Grand Rapids, MI: William B. Eerdmans Publishing Company, 1999).

rationalistic, deductive, and linear approach to church life that some Evangelicals have taken during the modern era. It can be argued that after swallowing modernism completely, the evangelical Church lost a crucial sense of sacredness.

Dawn argues for a renewed sense of being the Church in its most basic purpose: worshipping God. This worship will have no other value or purpose other than to glorify the Triune God. Though there is constant temptation and pressure to make the Church's worship do something or be something for some sake other than purely worshipping, Christians must resist this Satanic magnetic pull and refrain from using worldly trained skills to make the worship accomplish something other than "wasting" time with God.

There is a strange yet popular idea today of making worship into an evangelistic endeavor. The theory is as follows: invite the unconverted person into a worship service, and, as he experiences the "presence of God," he will be converted. Dawn addresses this misguided, experientially-based, Gnostic-like program in her other book, *Reaching Out Without Dumbing Down.*[35] Another troubling trend is to see worship as a means to the end of "bringing people into the presence of God." This of course misses the biblical point that one is always in God's presence and again uses worship as a device to create a self-centered, subjective experience. One more strange development in worship today is the emergence of the nonleading leader. In many postmodern churches, the musician at the front may be having his own little personal worship experience, which the congregation is invited to join in on if it knows the tune. There is very little "leadership" in this. It fits the postmodern, individualistic, private religious desires of those who want the common church experience that is a popular replacement today for authentic Christian worship. But it is not authentic *pathos*. The postmodern context offers us many strange and enticing ways to substitute authentic Christian worship for entertaining, exciting, selfishly fulfilling experiences.

---

35   Marva J. Dawn, Reaching Out Without Dumbing Down: A Theology of Worship for These Urgent Times (Grand Rapids, MI: William B. Eerdmans Publishing Company, 1995).

The Church must guard against conforming to the patterns of this or any era. God does not change, and his mandate for the Church remains the same. Authentic Christian Spiritual formation comes through careful listening to and proclamation of the *logos* of the Word of God, in the *ethos* of our contemporary context, with valid *pathos*. During the writing of this chapter, Stanley Grenz died suddenly. One of his last interviews contained this answer to a question about his thoughts on the next twenty-five years of the Church in this postmodern setting. He said,

> As I look to the future I am profoundly hopeful— not because of what I believe we will accomplish, but because of the God in whom I believe. Although the problems we face are enormous, we stand under the mandate of Jesus Christ who is the Lord of Creation. We are indwelt by the Holy Spirit. And, we are children of the Creator of the universe. For this reason, I am convinced that just as the gospel has gone forth with power in every era and to every generation, so also the gospel will sound forth in the postmodern context in which we live. And the God who promises to bring creation to its divinely intended goal invites us to participate in the divine program. May we, therefore, empowered by the Spirit, be faithful to the mandate Christ has entrusted to us, to the glory of God![36]

One will do well to heed these words as one endeavors to be God's faithful steward, listening to his *logos*—exegeting it, believing it, and living it with authentic *pathos*—and truly exposing it to the genuine *ethos* of this postmodern generation.

---

36   Rogier Bos' interview with Stan Grenz was first published in May 1999 issue of Next-Wave Magazine. It was republished online at http://www.the-next-wave.org/ stories/storyReader$607 following Dr. Grenz's death on March 12, 2005.

Chapter 2
The Content of Spiritual Formation

The Posture of Listening to God's Word

The following chapter is an attempt to articulate a biblical theology for an authentic definition and approach to the content of Christian Spiritual formation for every generation. It can be demonstrated that this formation has always been shaped through the public proclamation of the texts of the Holy Scriptures. Preaching can be seen throughout the panorama of the entire story of God's redemptive history, recorded in the Scriptures, as the greatest work of the shepherds of God's flock. In the following chapter, I will demonstrate that authentic Christian preaching, in every generation, has always been the act of God's representative messenger, paying attention to the *logos* of God's revealed Word and proclaiming the meaning of God's Word to the people in their contemporary context. The leaders of Christian communities must give precedence to the text of God's Word and defer to it for the authority and context of their messages. They must preach the Word. They must not begin with themselves. They must read the text, exegete it, understand it, and proclaim it to their gathered audience, in their language, history, and culture. They must then apply it to their existential reality.

God wants to form us, reform us, and transform us. He formed all that is. He has been reforming a people for himself through all of history. He is transforming individuals to fit them into his reformed humanity. This is a Spiritual formation, and it comes through his revealed Word.

God has shown himself to be a God of revelation. This does not mean that he has revealed all knowledge, but merely that he has chosen to initiate the revelation of his nature and his will himself by initiating revelatory speech.[37] God initiates, and his people respond. God speaks; his people listen. As Alister McGrath points out,

> "Revelation" does not mean merely the transmission of a body of knowledge, but the personal self-disclosure of God within history. God has taken the initiative through a process of self-disclosure, which reaches its climax and fulfillment in the history of Jesus of Nazareth.[38]

God's self-revelation is his Word. His Word created everything. His Word came to his chosen people, through his chosen leaders. His Word to and through his chosen prophets was recorded and regarded as Scripture. Later, his Word became flesh and lived for a while among us. This Word was witnessed and proclaimed by the Apostles.[39] The people of God are the people who come together to listen to the Word of God.[40] God's Word defines them. It draws God's people into relationship with him. As Eugene Peterson writes,

> The very essence of "word" is personal. It is the means by which what is within one person is shared

37   H. Richard Niebuhr points out that by "revelation," we must mean more than just the "historic Jesus" (Barth) or the egocentric "self" (Descartes). We must mean the centrally radiating reality of a revealing, eternal God. The Meaning of Revelation (New York, NY: Macmillan Publishing Company, 1960), 111.
38   Alister McGrath, Christian Theology : An Introduction (Oxford, UK: Blackwell Publishers, 1994), 153.
39   I will capitalize the word "Apostle" when referring to a member of the inner circle of men chosen directly by Jesus, including Paul, or these men as a group, and to that which belongs to them.
40   It was Rev. David Short (St. John's Shaughnessy Anglican Church, Vancouver, BC) whom I first heard use this phrase. In 1995 he said, "The definition of the people of God is the people who gather to listen to the Word of God read, sung, prayed, and preached. We then go out and worship God the rest of the week with our lives."

with another person. Words link spirits.… When a word is spoken and heard, it joins speaker and hearer into a whole relationship.… The intent of revelation is not to inform us about God but to involve us in God.[41]

The primary role of the Christian leader, then, ought to be to lead people to pay attention to God's initiating revelatory speech. The leader must position God's people to a place and posture of receiving God's Word. Paul Barnett points out that the role of God's leader is often described as that of a "shepherd" who leads God's flock (Num. 27:15–18, 2 Sam. 5:1–4, Jer. 3:15, 23:4, Jer. 50:6–7, Ezek. 34:23, Zech. 10:2–3, John 21:17, Acts 20:28, 1 Pet. 5:2 NIV).[42]

God is not in some faraway country, to which leaders must take the flock of the people of God. Rather, he is the radiating center of all existence. God is ever present and ever revealing. The Christian leader's task is to help people pay attention to God's self-revelation. This is not a matter of humans initiating searches or opinions about God, but an active leading of God's people to listen to God's personally initiated revelation to his people and his Word. A leader does not gather God's people to listen to his ideas about God, but to listen to God revealing himself.

It is essential that leaders begin by being formed themselves by listening to God's Word through careful exegesis and study, and that they publicly direct their congregations in such a way that the Word is heard regularly and clearly. The act of preaching cannot merely be a lecture of human opinion. It must be more than a talk from a topical series on people's perceived needs. It surely moves beyond the repetition of introductory evangelism or apologetics. It ought never to be the simplistic reciting of legalistic platitudes that uses God's Word as merely an encyclopedia of morality, nor ought it ever be an Ouija board-like use of Scripture for the spiritualistic practice of personal,

---

41   Eugene Peterson, Reversed Thunder (San Francisco, CA: HarperCollins Publishers, 1988), 12–13.

42   This idea was taken from notes from the course The Lost Art of Preaching taught by Paul Barnett and David Short at Regent College, Vancouver, BC, in 1999.

esoteric experience.[43] The first and most important principle must be the fundamental posture of any leader of God's people to see himself, above anything else, as leading God's people to pay attention to God's radiating revelation.[44] God's revelation must be set as the center of attention, rather than all of the competing human centers, which call for attention both inside and outside the Church.

The Leading of God's People to Pay Attention to God's Word

Any theological foundation for a framework of understanding the essential primacy of Christian leaders to lead from the centrality of the texts of Christian Holy Scripture must be founded on and found

43   Eugene Peterson writes that two of the greatest enemies of the Christian faith are (and always have been) moralism: "dishonoring the Son" (or legalism) and gnosticism: "dishonoring the Father" (or "spiritualism"). The third enemy that he identified was sectarianism: "dishonoring the Spirit" in Christ Plays in Ten Thousand Places (Winnipeg, MB: CMBC Publications, 1999). He writes, "Gnosticism" is a virus in the bloodstream of religion and keeps resurfacing every generation or so advertised as brand new, replete with a new brand name. On examination, though, it turns out to be the same old thing but with a new public relations agency" (page 32). And later, "moralism works from a base of human ability and arranges life in such a way that my good behavior will guarantee protection from punishment or disaster. Moralism works from strength, not weakness. Moralism uses God (or the revelation of God) in order not to need God any longer. Moral codes are used as stepping stones to independence from God" (page 48). When Susan Wise Bauer wrote her review of the two new books on the life of King David by Eugene Peterson (Leap Over A Wall: Earthy Spirituality for Everyday Christians, San Francisco, CA: HarperCollins Publishers, 1997) and Chuck Swindoll (David: A Man of Passion and Destiny, Waco, TX: Word Books Publishers, 1997), she made note that the major difference between the two books was that Peterson took the story of David seriously as scriptural narrative, while Swindoll reduced the story (and the Scriptures) to a set of moralisms. She writes, "topology creeps into Swindoll's stories: David's life is a series of moral lessons … to flatten story into principle takes away a vital dimension of revelation." Susan Wise Bauer, "A Paper Doll King David: More than a Tale with a Moral" in Christianity Today (June 16, 1997), 42.

44   Getting the center right is the essential act of the Christian life. This is the fundamental theological issue. This is far more primary and vital than any preaching techniques. As John Stott writes, "the essential secret is not mastering certain techniques but being mastered by certain convictions. In other words, theology is more important than methodology." Between Two Worlds: The Challenge of Preaching Today (Grand Rapids, MI: William B. Eerdmans Publishing Company), 92.

in the revealed Word. There are many places one could look within God's written Word to find a framework for this picture of setting proper attention on the radiating centrality of God's initiating revelation rather than on human initiative. One excellent text to use is the concluding book of the canon of the Bible. The picture of God at the center, radiating his revelation out from that center to the outer edges of the cosmos, can be perceived in the picture John gives in Revelation. Chapters four and five apocalyptically describe the expanding circles of God's personal, revealing initiative being manifested.[45]

It can be argued that John, writing "on the Lord's day" (Rev. 1:10 NIV), is imagining himself worshipping with members of his seven congregations on Sunday,[46] listening to God's Word. He reminds them of their common bond and center: the Lord Jesus, who is the Word made visible (Rev. 1:7–8). After he turns "to see the voice that was speaking" (Rev. 1:12 NIV), he writes to each of his seven congregations the revealing Word from God, ending each revelation with the charge, "he who has an ear, let him hear what the Spirit says to the churches" (Rev. 2:7, 2:11, 2:17, 2:29, 3:6, 3:13, 3:22 NIV).

One theory of the pattern of the whole letter of John's Revelation argues that the seventh revelation introduces the next cycle in the series of revelations.[47] Before the common refrain ("he who has an ear…") comes at the end of the revelation to the church in Laodicea,

---

45   Eugene Peterson points out in Reversed Thunder (San Francisco, CA: HarperCollins Publishers, 1988) that the title Apokalupsis literally means "to take the lid off/to reveal." Peterson has taught elsewhere that "we don't figure things out. We are shown. We assume salvation and revelation. It is not private but openly presented. It is historic truth, God in history. As the Hebrews wrote history, the covenant became the syntax of their language…. Rather than making it up, they were waiting to be told." Ministry and Spirituality class lectures, Regent College, Vancouver, BC, 1994.

46   See W. Scott's notes on "the Lord's Day" in New Testament Studies, vol. 12 (1965), 70–75, as well as Ignatius' letter to the Magnesians 9 and the Didache 14.

47   According to the progressive parallelism view of "The Revelation," the letter consists of a cycle of seven depictions of the revelation of the Word, Jesus to the church, and the world from the time of his first coming to the time of his second coming. This view is explained best by William Hendrickson in his More Than Conquerors, 2nd. ed. (Grand Rapids, MI: Baker Books, 1940), 22–64.

John introduces the picture of the "open door" (Rev. 3:20 NIV). Jesus says,

> Here I am! I stand at the door and knock. If anyone hears my voice and opens the door, I will come in and eat with him, and he with me. To him who overcomes, I will give the right to sit with me on my throne, just as I overcame and sat down with my Father on his throne (Rev. 3:30–21 NIV).

The reference to the seven golden lamp stands (Rev. 1:12–13) evokes the intimate and immediate presence of God in the holy place of the Tabernacle (Exod. 25:37–40). It can be argued that John sees his seven congregations as the instruments of light before the great light of the throne of God. John's little, scattered congregations can be seen, like all members of God's covenant worshipping people, as always before the throne of God, receiving his revealing Word.

Who can enter into the center of God's holy throne, his intimate presence? The answer is the one who "hears my voice and opens the door" (Rev. 3:20 NIV). How is his voice heard and how is that door opened? John immediately answers this question. The next thing John describes is "a door standing open in heaven" (Rev. 4:1 NIV). God opens that door. He says, "Come up here and I will show you what must take place after this" (Rev. 4:1 NIV). God initiates the very possibility of a relationship with him. It is an invitation to commune with the very community of God. The triune God (the Spirit, the Word, and the One on the throne) invites John into his presence to experience relationship with him. John writes,

> I looked, and there before me was a door standing open in heaven. And the voice I had first heard speaking to me like a trumpet said, "Come up here, and I will show you what must take place after this." At once I was in the Spirit, and there before me was a throne in heaven with someone sitting on it (Rev. 4:1–2 NIV).

This is the regular experience of the community of God's covenant people who come together to listen to the Word of God "on the Lord's day." John goes on to describe the regular experience of relationship with God through worship and God's revelation. God says, "I will show you what is to happen next" (Rev. 4:2 NIV). John then describes a picture of what happens "next,"[48] every time Christians assemble to pay attention to the radiating Word of God.

The Church is centered on the revealing, living God, not on herself or on her individual members. Like concentric circles, God's revealing Word radiates outward. John sees "a throne in heaven with someone sitting on it" (Rev. 4:2 NIV). This is the central person of God who is on his throne.[49] From this center, God reveals himself to the cosmos that he has created and that he sustains through his Word. He has "the appearance of jasper and carnelian. A rainbow, resembling an emerald, encircled the throne" (Rev. 4:3 NIV). Like the gleam of precious jewels, God's light is refracted out from his encircled center.

The Radiating, Revealing Word in Creation

Beginning with creation, God has initiated his formative revelation to the world by speaking his Word. His interaction with the world and his people comes at his command. At creation he spoke his Word into the void, and the cosmos leapt into being (Ps. 33:6–9, 2 Pet. 3:5). His Word commands and sustains the natural forces (Ps.

---

48   According to Keil and Delitzch (Commentary on the Old Testament, volume 9 (Daniel), 111), the phrase "what must take place after this" is found in the LXX of Daniel 2:29, 45 where it means "next" in chronological time, immediately from the time of the writing, rather than some future time.

49   Alan Johnson writes, "Chapter four is above all a vision of the royal throne of God … the source of all that will happen on earth. It will all be an expression of the throne's purpose; nothing happens, nothing exists in the past, present, or future apart from God's intention.... The throne symbolizes God's majesty and power." Revelation: The Expositor's Bible Commentary vol. 12 (Grand Rapids, MI: Zondervan, 1981), 462.

104:7, Ps. 119:89–90, Heb. 1:3). In the very fabric of this created cosmos, his essence is "manifested" (Rom. 1:19 NIV). He first revealed himself through what he has created. It can be argued that John is describing the revealing creation, represented by the wild creature (lion), the domesticated creature (ox), the human creature (man), and the creature of the heavens (eagle). These are seen at the center, around the throne, looking both ways, to the throne and out to the cosmos, worshipping and speaking (paying attention to the center and proclaiming out to the cosmos).

> In the center, around the throne, were four living creatures, and they were covered with eyes, in front and in back. The first living creature was like a lion, the second was like an ox, the third had a face like a man, the fourth was like a flying eagle. Each of the four living creatures had six wings and was covered with eyes all around, even under his wings. Day and night they never stop saying: "Holy, holy, holy is the Lord God Almighty, who was, and is, and is to come" (Rev. 4:6–8 NIV).

The Radiating Revelation of God through Men

The next consecutive circle of God's radiating formative revelation comes through his chosen spokespersons to his covenant people, recorded in the Scriptures.

> Surrounding the throne were twenty-four other thrones, and seated on them were twenty-four elders. They were dressed in white and had crowns of gold on their heads (Rev. 4:4 NIV).

After God spoke the world into being, he spoke to and through his chosen spokespersons. This may be the symbolism of the twenty-four elders.[50] The Word of God was first spoken to and then through his chosen spokespersons, bringing clarity to the vague natural revelation of creation. It can be demonstrated that this "special revelation" in history came to and through six primary kinds of "witnesses." These six formative witnesses were patriarchs, a lawgiver, judges, prophets, wise ones, and Apostles. Their testimony was recorded in the written Word of God (the Bible). Each of these types of "preachers" led God's covenant people by first listening to the content of God's Word themselves, understanding it, and then declaring it to their contemporary generation in their language, culture, and history.[51]

1. The Patriarchs

God first formed and spoke directly to and with the patriarchs. He walked in the garden with Adam (Gen. 3:8). He conversed with Noah and Abraham (Gen. 6:13, 12:1). He treated these men and their families with distinction. He uniquely interacted with them, establishing and defining his covenant with them and their lineage. God initiated through his active speech (his Word), revealing to and through these consecrated men (and their families) his specific will and character. They were called into covenant with God and then called to be the leading figures of humanity, as mediators between man and God. It can be argued that their primary role was to listen to God's Word and to help others pay attention to him. Through them, God formed a people for himself.

---

50   It is difficult to identify the actual identity of the twenty-four elders. Michael Wilcock argues for their association with the twenty-four priestly divisions in 1 Chronicles 24, whose job it was to administer the ministries of the Temple worship. The Message of Revelation: I Saw Heaven Open (Leicester, UK: Inter-Varsity Press, 1989), 61.

51   Dr. Tom Cowan makes this case in his unpublished doctoral thesis, Preaching Biblical Truth in a Postmodern Culture (Western Seminary, Portland, OR, 1997).

2a. The Lawgiver

Next, God called the Lawgiver, Moses, who also had a unique relationship with God. In spite of Moses' protests, God initiated a special relationship with him, revealing a greater depth of knowledge of God's nature, name, and will (Exod. 3). Moses can be seen as a transition figure, being a kind of patriarch and a kind of prophet. But Moses is also the *only* Lawgiver (John 1:17, Heb. 3). After revealing himself through creation, and then in covenant with specific humans, God revealed himself one step further and deeper through the Exodus, the Mosaic Law, the Levitical code, and the new theocratic covenant community, Israel. Moses, as the mediator between God and the faith community, was primarily called to lead God's covenant people to listen to God's Word.

> Then Moses went up to God, and the LORD called to him from the mountain and said, "This is what you are to say to the house of Jacob and what you are to tell the people of Israel: 'You yourselves have seen what I did to Egypt, and how I carried you on eagles' wings and brought you to myself. Now if you obey me fully and keep my covenant, then out of all nations you will be my treasured possession. Although the whole earth is mine, you will be for me a kingdom of priests and a holy nation.' These are the words you are to speak to the Israelites" (Exod. 19:3–6 NIV).

The whole community was gathered before the mountain and waited for God's Word. God spoke to Moses and then appointed Moses to speak his Word to Israel for him. Israel's formation and transformation was God's initiative. And, though "the whole earth is [his]," God wants his covenant faith community to be a "kingdom of priests and a holy nation." God does not need human help. However, he forms his people through his personal initiated revelation to them through his Word. Then he reforms them to be his ministers, administrating his Word to the world, leading the rest of humanity to be transformed towards the truly human posture of listening: to hear his Word and respond in proper worship.

> So Moses went back and summoned the elders of the people and set before them all the words the LORD had commanded him to speak. The people all responded together, "We will do everything the LORD has said." So Moses brought their answer back to the LORD. The LORD said to Moses, "I am going to come to you in a dense cloud, so that the people will hear me speaking with you and will always put their trust in you" (Exod. 19:7–9a NIV).

In the next part of Revelation, the Apostle John evokes this historic picture, borrowing the imagery from Exodus 19, to link what "will happen next" (the immediate experience of the worshipping faith community whenever the Church gathers as God's people to listen to his Word) with what happened when God's people gathered at Mount Sinai.

> On the morning of the third day there was thunder and lightning, with a thick cloud over the mountain, and a very loud trumpet blast. Everyone in the camp trembled. Then Moses led the people out of the camp to meet with God, and they stood at the foot of the mountain. Mount Sinai was covered with smoke, because the LORD descended on it in fire. The smoke billowed up from it like smoke from a furnace, the whole mountain trembled violently, and the sound of the trumpet grew louder and louder. Then Moses spoke and the voice of God answered him (Exod. 19:16–19 NIV).

The people of God come together to be formed by listening to the Word of God and then go out to worship God by communicating and demonstrating the transformative revelation of God to the world. This was true of Israel at Mount Sinai, and it was true of the seven churches John wrote his "Revelation" to. It is also true of the authentic Christian faith community today. The essential task of God's appointed Spiritual leader has always been to help the faith community to be the authentic people of God, to help them gather to listen to the Word of God, and then to go out and worship God by being part of the "kingdom of priests and a holy nation" (Exod. 19:6).

2b. The Priests, the Sacraments, and the Artists

During this time, the ceremonial function of the institutional priesthood was established. One could say that the purpose of the Levitical priesthood was to complement the role of the Law in the transformative life of the community. Artists were also enlisted by God to be a part of his public revelation in and through the faith community. Artists constructed all of the elements of the Tabernacle in the wilderness (Exod. 25:3–30:10). Bezalel and Oholiab were specifically called and equipped by God (Exod. 31:1–6) to be his formative instruments of revelation. Artists were sent from Tyre to build a palace for David in Jerusalem (2 Sam. 5:11–12). It can be argued that artists were enlisted as "prophets" through music and song in the assembly (1 Chron. 25). Artists were also employed in the building of God's temple (2 Chron. 2–4). The Tabernacle and the Temple and all that was seen, heard, touched, smelled, and tasted in them were complementary elements to the revelation of God's Word. These can be understood as visible expository sermons, sacramentally exposing the person and will of him who is at the center, on the throne.

The ritual practices of the sacramental community can be understood as the visual sermons of the people of God.[52] The Levitical

---

52   John Stott writes, "Augustine's designation of the sacraments as 'visible words' (verba visibilia) supplies an essential clue to their function and value. They too speak. Both Word and sacrament bear witness to Christ.... The ministry of Word and sacrament is a single ministry, the Word proclaiming and the sacraments dramatizing God's promises. Yet the Word is primary, since without it the sign becomes dark in meaning,

code was a communal response to God's revelation. God not only initiated the revelation of his person and will and his redemptive relationship between himself and man, he also created a practice of living the reality of that relationship through everyday practice of formative worship, sacrifices, and ceremony. This is the authentic action of the faith community.

> Also before the throne there was what looked like a sea of glass, clear as crystal.... Whenever the living creatures give glory, honor and thanks to him who sits on the throne and who lives for ever and ever, the twenty-four elders fall down before him who sits on the throne, and worship him who lives for ever and ever. They lay their crowns before the throne and say: "You are worthy, our Lord and God, to receive glory and honor and power, for you created all things, and by your will they were created and have their being" (Rev. 4:6, 9–11 NIV).

The authentic act of response to God's revelation is worship (Exod. 4:29–31). Worship must not be used as a tool to try to obtain revelation, or as a self-centered, esoteric experiential device.[53] It must always and only be a genuine response to what God has revealed. As God's self-initiated revelation is received, his people respond in prayer, praise, and proclamation. They lay whatever crowns they possess at his throne, declaring the truth that God has revealed to themselves, each other, and the world.

The Christian sacraments can also be understood as expository sermons. God's truth is revealed through the acted-out expositions of baptism and communion. Paul declares, "For whenever you eat

---

if not actually dumb" (Between Two Worlds, 114).

53   Marva J. Dawn makes the convincing point in her book that "worship" is not meant to "accomplish" anything in this world. "Worshipping the Lord is—in the world's eyes—a waste of time. It is indeed, a royal waste of time, but a waste of time nonetheless. By engaging in it, we don't accomplish anything useful in our society's terms." A Royal "Waste" Of Time: The Splendor of Worshiping God and Being Church for the World (Grand Rapids, MI: William B. Eerdmans Publishing Company, 1999), 1.

this bread and drink this cup, you proclaim the Lord's death until he comes" (1 Cor. 11:26). And, as Peter points out, "This water symbolizes baptism that now saves you also—not the removal of dirt from the body but the pledge of a good conscience toward God (1 Pet. 3:21). These outward signs of inward realities are symbolic proclamations of God's revelation.[54] Lutheran professor Gordon Lathrop, commenting on one of the earliest "*ordos*" of Christian sacramental practice, found in St. Ignatius, literally calls the water of baptism "the speaking water."[55]

Returning to John's "Revelation," one can argue that John is describing this same understanding of Sunday worship as responsive, expository sacrament. Through the visible preaching of baptism (the crystal sea 4:6) and the eucharistic preaching of his sacrificial death (the slaughtered lamb 5:6), the good news of God's Word is exposed. As well as these sacraments, the public and private Scripture reading and meditating (the text scroll 5:1), the allegiance to Jesus (the Lion of Judah, the triumphal root of David 5:5), the regular public practice of praise (harp 5:8), prayer (incense 5:8), and preaching (the messengers 5:11), the Holy of Holies before the throne of God is entered. Only God the Word can open the "seal" and reveal himself, the Word. No one else can open the "scroll or even look inside it" (5:3 NIV).

3. The Judges

After Moses, there was a series of judges to whom God spoke, and through whom God formatively spoke to the covenant community. God continued to initiate the revelation of his nature and will by

---

54   Alister McGrath points out that for both Melanchthon (Propositions on the Mass, 1521) and Luther (The Blessed Sacrament of the Holy and True Body of Christ, 1519 and The Babylonian Captivity of the Church, 1520) the two protestant sacraments (baptism and the Lord's Supper) are visible signs of the spoken promises of God, meant to remind and instruct the faithful in what God has declared. Christian Theology: An Introduction (Oxford, UK, Blackwell Publishers, 1994), 433–439.
55   Gordon W. Lathrop. Holy People: A Liturgical Ecclesiology (Minneapolis, MN: Fortress Press, 1999), 135

speaking his Word through these judges. It can be argued that the primary role of these judges was to speak for God by exegeting God's Law and applying the authentic content of the Law to the specific existential context of the everyday life of the faith community. It is not enough to simply proclaim God's Word randomly to the people of God. Authentic Christian leadership requires leading God's people to specific application of God's revelation to the real experience of Spiritual formation toward godly living.

The second chapter of Judges reveals God's plan for the post-Moses/Joshua task of authentic Spiritual leadership. After Joshua died, "another generation grew up, who knew neither the LORD nor what he had done for Israel" (Judg. 2:10b NIV). They became ignorant of the salvation history of God, recorded in the Law of Moses, so they "did evil in the eyes of the LORD and served the Baals. They forsook the LORD, the God of their fathers, who had brought them out of Egypt. They followed and worshiped various gods of the peoples around them. They provoked the LORD to anger because they forsook him and served Baal and the Ashtoreths" (Judg. 2:11–13 NIV). Because no one taught them the Word of God, they could not obey it. They were unaware of the texts of God's recorded revelation. Thus they were not Spiritually formed. The result of not hearing the Word of God was that "whenever Israel went out to fight, the hand of the LORD was against them to defeat them, just as he had sworn to them" (Judg. 2:15 NIV). He had sworn it to them in the text of the Law, but they were ignorant of God's warnings and promises because no one was preaching the text to them. So "the LORD raised up judges, who saved them out of the hands of these raiders" (Judg. 2:16 NIV). The primary task of the judges was to lead the people of God to listen to the text of God. This was a preaching task.

> Yet they would not listen to their judges but prostituted themselves to other gods and worshiped them. Unlike their fathers, they quickly turned from the way in which their fathers had walked, the way of obedience to the LORD's commands. Whenever

the LORD raised up a judge for them, he was with the judge and saved them out of the hands of their enemies as long as the judge lived.… But when the judge died, the people returned to ways even more corrupt than those of their fathers, following other gods and serving and worshiping them. They refused to give up their evil practices and stubborn ways. Therefore the LORD was very angry with Israel and said, "Because this nation has violated the covenant that I laid down for their forefathers and has not listened to me, I will no longer drive out before them any of the nations Joshua left when he died" (Judg. 2:17–21 NIV).

God intended these men and women to be listened to, and what they were to be listened to about was "the way of obedience to the LORD's commands" and "the covenant that [God] laid down for their forefathers," his recorded Word. This is how they were to be Spiritually formed. This is what Deborah the prophetess (preacher)[56]

56　According to Hobart E. Freeman, the essential idea in the word nevi'a, used here to describe Deborah's function, "is that of authorized spokesman. Interpreters have found the basic thought, not in the etymology, which is lost in the dust of antiquity, but in the general usage of the word and in three Pentateuchal loci. The first locus follows the last of Moses' famous objections to being God's designated spokesman to the children of Israel and to Pharaoh (Exod. 6:28–30). 'And the Lord said unto Moses, See, I have made thee as God to Pharaoh; and Aaron thy brother shall be thy prophet. Thou shalt speak all that I command thee; and Aaron thy brother shall speak unto Pharaoh' (Exod. 7:1,2). Whatever the origin of the word, therefore, a nābi' is a person authorized to speak for another, for Aaron, speaking in Moses' place to Pharaoh, is Moses' nābi'. The second locus follows an incident wherein Aaron and Miriam had presumed to supplant Moses as mediator of the divine revelation to themselves (Num. 12:1–2). The Lord himself then intervened by declaring that Moses only would hold direct conversation with the Almighty, that he would, however, communicate with prophets by dreams and visions (Num. 12:4–8). What is left unstated, but is presumed and stated clearly elsewhere (e.g. Jer. 23) is that a genuine nābi' could be such a spokesman for God only if God had genuinely given him a message (however obscurely) to speak. The third occurs just before the great legislator's death. In view of the end of 'face-to-face' communications from God through Moses, there was a formal announcement of the office of nābi' on a continuing basis. In this passage (Deut. 18:9–14) Jehovah formally proscribed any traffic with the bogus pagan mantic practices of Canaan (Deut. 18:9–14). Then having stated that a line of prophets would speak (or write) with the same was doing as she held court "under the Palm of Deborah" (Judg. 4:4 NIV).[57] The Law by which she judged was the recorded text of the Law of Moses. Gideon only knew how to "build a proper kind of altar to the LORD" (Judg. 6:26 NIV) because he paid attention to the texts of the Law of Moses. Abimelech demonstrates his knowledge of the texts of the Word of God when he scatters salt over the conquered city of Shechem (Judg. 9:45).[58] When the people

---

authority that Moses had spoken (and written), he commanded the Israelites to render the prophet the same obedience (Deut. 18:15,18–19) which he had commanded them to give to Moses. Five certifying signs of a prophet (Ps. 74:9; cf. Matt. 12:38; Acts 2:22) were announced as follows: 1) the prophet must be Israelite, 'of thy brethren' (vv. 15, 18); 2) he speaks in Jehovah's name, 'voice of Jehovah' (v. 16) 'he shall speak in my name' (v. 19; cf. v. 20), death being the penalty for false claims to so speak (v. 20, cf. Deut. 18:1 ff.; 1 Kings 18:20–40); 3) supernatural knowledge of the near future was to be a sign of the authenticity of divine appointment (vv. 21–22; cf. 1 Kings 22; Jer. 28, esp. v. 17); 4) the prophet might perform some other miraculous sign (see Deut. 13:1 ff.; cf. 1 Kings 18:24; and esp. v. 36); and 5) the final test is strict conformity to (agreement with) the previously certified revelations, by Moses at first and by the prophets to follow (Deut. 13:1–18). The fifth requirement is emphatic, the entire thirteenth chapter being devoted to it. Hebrews 1:1–2 clearly declares that the entire OT is a deposit of written oracles of the ne bi' îm. The word 'prophets' is extremely important in this text, for, in the LXX nābi' is always translated prophets; there is not a single instance of any other word (TDNT, V1, p. 812). Once in a text wherein the ages-long work of the line of authentic prophets is summarized, the OT uses the word mal'āk 'messenger,' 'angel.' The LXX gives the proper sense by using aggelos (2 Chron. 36:15)." Theological Wordbook of the Old Testament, Vol. 2 (Chicago, IL: Moody Press, 1980), 546–547. As John A. Broadus asserted, "The prophets were preachers." Quoted in A History of Preaching by Edwin C. Dargan (Grand Rapids, MI: Baker Book House, 1968) p. 19

57   According to Herbert Wolf, "The palm is associated with prosperity in Psalm 92:12 and leadership in Isaiah 9:14." Judges: The Expositor's Bible Commentary, volume 3 (Grand Rapids, MI.: Zondervan, 1981), 404.

58   The symbolism of Abimelech's act is clearly associated with the curses promised by God in Scripture upon those "whose heart turns away from the Lord our God to go and worship the gods of other nations" after he "hears the words of this oath.... [His] whole land will be a burning waste of salt and sulfur—nothing planted, nothing sprouting, no vegetation growing on it. It will be like the destruction of Sodom and Gomorrah, Admah and Zeboiim, which the LORD overthrew in fierce anger. All the nations will ask: 'Why has the LORD done this to this land? Why this fierce, burning anger?' And the answer will be: 'It is because this people abandoned the covenant of the LORD, the God of their fathers, the covenant he made with them when he brought them out of Egypt. They went off and worshiped other gods and bowed down to them, gods they did not know, gods he had not given them. Therefore the LORD's anger burned against this land, so that he brought on it all the curses written in this book'"

of God listened to their leaders, who preached the Word of God, they prospered. When they ignored the Word, they were cursed. Jephthah demonstrates his attention to the Law of Moses in his response to the Ammonite King, quoting the texts of the existent Scriptures (Judg. 11:14–27).

Here, the formation of God's people through listening to God's Word by paying attention to God's text is seen. By the time of the judges, the Law was recorded. Through the stories of the lives and words of the judges came more Scripture. The fundamental work of listening to God, from the time of Moses on, became the careful exegesis and proclamation of God's text.[59] This text is variously called, among many things, "the Scriptures" (Mark 12:10); the "law," "decrees," "statutes," "commands," "precepts," and "promises" (Ps. 119); "the law and the prophets" (Luke16:16); "the apostles and prophets" (Eph. 2:20); "my word" (Isa. 55:11); "the word of God" (1 Thess. 2:13); "the word of the prophets" (2 Pet. 1:19); and "the word of truth" (Col. 1:5).

From the time of Moses on, there was a holy text to pay attention to and to meditate on. Authentic godly meditation is precisely what the Hebrew word for meditation evokes—a "mumbling over" of God's revealed (written) Word.[60] When the Lord tells Joshua to "not

---

(Deut. 29:18–19, 23–27 NIV).

59   Exegesis demands careful, rigorous study of the texts of God's Word in their original languages. John Stott writes, "The higher our view of the Bible, the more pains-
taking and conscientious our study of it should be. If this book is indeed the Word of
God, then away with slovenly, slipshod exegesis! We have to make time to penetrate the
text until it yields up its treasures. Only when we have ourselves absorbed its message,
can we confidently share it with others. God spoke to Samuel when he listened to him;
then, when Samuel spoke to Israel, they listened to him (1 Sam. 3:9–4:1). Similarly,
before Ezekiel was in a position to speak God's Word to the people, he had to devour
and digest it. God said to him: "Son of man … eat this scroll, and go, speak to the
house of Israel" (Ezek. 3:1), (Between Two Worlds, 182). Tom Cowan (Lambrick Park
Church, Victoria, BC) tells of an incident he experienced while teaching an advanced
preaching class to a group of pastors from a particular denomination. These pastors
were almost all graduate school trained, full-time employed preachers. When Cowan
wrote some preliminary Biblical texts, in Greek, on the board for discussion, no one
could read them. It came to light that none of the pastors in the class ever did exegetical
work in the original languages of the texts they preached on each week. Most of them
rarely, if ever, used grammatical-historical aids.
60   The Brown-Driver-Briggs Hebrew and English Lexicon defines the word hagah

let this book of the Law depart from your mouth; meditate on it day and night" (Josh. 1:8), God was instructing him to memorize and "mumble over" the text day and night. When the last psalm before the psalms of ascent (Ps. 119) asks, "How can a young man keep his way pure?" the answer is proclaimed, "by living according to your Word.... I have hidden your Word in my heart.... With my lips I recount all the laws that come from your mouth" (Ps. 119:9, 11).

When one is doing this, it is imperative that it is done with a thorough understanding of the context of the passages being meditated on. It is so easy for people, as fallen, self-centered creatures, to misinterpret the texts and apply them in unholy ways to self-centered contexts. Joshua and the writer of Psalm 119 were steeped in an understanding of the content, context, history, and meaning of the texts they prayed, memorized, and mumbled over. The Apostle John wrote Revelation with this same Scripture-soaked imagination, drawing from the imagery of the whole revealed Word, and quoting from almost every book of the Bible.

Some have argued that there are two contrasting approaches to the understanding of the Word. One is the rational, exegetical study of the Scriptures with one's mind, while the other is the direct, inspirational revelation of the Spirit of God to one's heart. It is said that one represents the ministry of the Word and the other the ministry of the Spirit. John Woodhouse makes a convincing argument for the absurdity of this dichotomy, stressing that the Word and the Spirit are inseparable.[61] He rejects the attempt to bring a "balance" between these two heretical extremes, demonstrating

---

(to meditate) as "moan, growl, utter, speak" (211). This is in direct contrast with the traditionally Eastern concept of "meditation," which is to empty one's mind of anything and to be esoterically transported to an alternative level of consciousness. This alternative version of "meditating" has been adopted in many "Christian" communities. Some leaders will even teach a kind of divination, wherein one is coached to "listen to the voice of God" through quiet listening techniques, and to divine feelings and impressions as God's special, private revelation. The Bible calls this practice "witchcraft" and forbids it (Deut. 18:9–13). It misses the point of the true spiritual exercise of "meditation," to mumble over, memorize, contemplate, and be shaped by the texts of God's written Word.

61   John Woodhouse, The Preacher and the Living Word (Leicester, UK: Inter-Varsity Press, 1995).

that the illumination of God's Word is the primary work and message of the Holy Spirit. He then calls for an embracing of the authentically Christian approach to the Word, which is a dynamic synergy between the Spirit of God speaking and working through the Word of God.

Others have argued that the Scriptures themselves cannot be considered clear enough for the preacher to give any kind of trustworthy interpretation of God's mysterious text. Mark Thompson has expertly defended the doctrine of the perspicuity of the Bible texts as they are studied in context and applied in the lives God calls his people to.[62] The biblical texts are clear, and they are the trustworthy content for authentic Spiritual formation.

4. The Prophets and the Kings

Just as Moses was a hybrid of patriarch and prophet, linking two covenantal epochs, Samuel was the last judge and also the first person in the Old Testament named as a prophet after Moses. He also linked the epochs of the theocratic tribal community of Israel and the theocratic Kingdoms of Israel and Judah. As a prophet, Samuel was a new kind of mediator between the radiating, central revelation of God's nature and will, and the people of God.[63] Beginning with Samuel and King Saul, prophets and kings shared the tasks of representing God to the people, and the people to God. Sometimes, the power struggles between royal prerogative and prophetic application of God's revelation led to rifts between kings and prophets. This was usually because either the king or the prophet, or both, stopped paying attention to God's central, radiating revelation, and so stopped listening to God, thus ceasing to operate as an authentic representative of God to his people.

---

62   Mark D. Thompson, A Clear and Present Word: The Clarity of Scripture (Downers Grove, Ill : Inter-Varsity Press, 2006).
63   Klaus Bockmuehl comments: "The Israelites recognized Samuel as the established prophet of the Lord whose task it was to announce to them the word of the Lord" (1 Sam. 3:20, 9:27). Listening to the God who Speaks (Colorado Springs, CO: Helmers & Howard Publishers, 1990), 21.

Isaiah gives us a remarkable insight into the calling of a prophet:

> The Sovereign LORD has given me an instructed tongue, to know the word that sustains the weary. He wakens me morning by morning, wakens my ear to listen like one being taught. The Sovereign LORD has opened my ears, and I have not been rebellious; I have not drawn back (Isa. 50:4–5 NIV).

The prophet was one who had been "instructed," and continued practicing the daily discipline of the "morning by morning" study of the Word. He listened to the Word as "one being taught," and he did not "[draw] back" from his primary role. The primary role of the prophet was to prophesy (or preach) God's revealed Word.[64] This is what preaching has fundamentally always been—professing the properly received, exegeted, and applied Word of God. The prophets were expected to be formed through their understanding of God's Word through exegeting the Law (which was the only revealed text they had at that point), to hear God's Word afresh (as prophets, they received God's special revelation directly and personally [Amos 3:7]), and to profess God's Word so that the community of God would be Spiritually formed.

Prophets were forbidden to pass their opinions off as God's authoritative Word (Jer. 31:34). These are plainly called "lies" (Isa. 9:15), and false prophecy was punishable by death (Deut.13:5). They preached God's revealed Word to their contemporary context. The postmodern church needs preachers who know and understand God's Word (through excellent exegesis, meditation, and living), and who know and understand their own contemporary context, so that they can proclaim God's authentic Word to their generation.

It is important to point out that God himself attested to the authority of prophets (and Apostles) as his spokesmen by doing

---

64   It is interesting that J. B. Phillips translates the New Testament word prophaytas as "preach" (for example: 1 Cor. 12:28 Phillips).

miracles through them. These miracles were a sign by which God's covenant people could test whether anyone who claimed to speak for God was indeed called by God to speak for him and to bring revelation from his throne. This is important for today because many men and women claim to speak for God and even claim to be prophets and Apostles. One must ask anyone by what authority he or she claims to speak for God, and ask for proof (a "sign") of his or her authority. Even still, the Church is warned to beware of false teachers and prophets who can also produce miraculous signs (Deut. 13:1–5, Mark 13:22–23). The real test of any teaching will be that it does not compromise, contradict, or even add to what God has revealed through his Word (Gal. 1:6–9).

5. The Wise Ones

During the full epoch of the time of the prophets, the faith community created the wisdom literature of the Old Testament Scriptures as Holy Spirit-inspired response to God's revealed Law. Designated wise ones wrote application of God's revelation and response to God's action and Word.[65] These songs, poems, proverbs, and stories were accredited as Scripture by God's Holy Spirit, endorsed by God's designated authoritative representatives, embraced by the authentic faith community, and lived and prayed as a part of the formative sacramental life of God's people. Jesus and the Apostles also endorsed the wisdom literature of the Old Testament as authentically part of the revealed Word of God by quoting it and teaching from it. These "wise" artists are part of the representative scriptural concentric circle around the revealing center of God's throne.

---

65   Bockmuehl points out that "Glossa Ordinaria, the standard medieval commentary on the Bible, begins its interpretation of the Psalms with a general discussion of prophecy. In its view, the Psalms, especially the many Psalms ascribed to the anointed king, David, are a continuation of prophecy, and indeed a form of prophesy in which the extraordinary phemonena and circumstances of the earlier experience of 'vision' have given way to the unobtrusive inner illumination by the Holy Spirit" (Listening to the God who Speaks, 33).

There was a period of about four hundred years between the last prophetic Word of the Old Testament and the first apostolic Word of the New Testament. During this time, like the four hundred years of captivity in Egypt, the people of God experienced a dry season without any new Word from God. One picture of the authentic practice of preaching in the faithful covenant community, just before that inter-testamental period, is recorded in Nehemiah 8:

> All the people assembled as one man in the square before the Water Gate. They told Ezra the scribe to bring out the Book of the Law of Moses, which the LORD had commanded for Israel. So on the first day of the seventh month Ezra the priest brought the Law before the assembly … He read it aloud from daybreak till noon … in the presence of the men, women and others who could understand. And all the people listened attentively to the Book of the Law. Ezra the scribe stood on a high wooden platform built for the occasion.… All the people could see him because he was standing above them; and as he opened it, the people all stood up.… The Levites … instructed the people in the Law while the people were standing there. They read from the Book of the Law of God, making it clear and giving the meaning so that the people could understand what was being read.… Then all the people went away to eat and drink, to send portions of food and to celebrate with great joy, because they now understood the words that had been made known to them (Neh. 8:1–12 NIV).

Here the authentic practice of the people of God is seen as they gather to listen to the formative Word of God read, sung, prayed, and preached, and then go out and worship God with their lives. This event occurred in the fifth century BC, yet it is a model of Spiritual formation that could be contemporary with Moses through to Saint Paul, or with Saint Clement through to Martin Lloyd-Jones or any emergent leader today. The public proclamation of God's Holy Scriptures is the historically authentic way that God's Word continues to form, reform, and transform his people.

As in the historic case of the Josian reformation (2 Kings 22–23), the people of God gather, and God's book is brought out. It is read aloud. They listen. God's leader (who has been formed himself through listening to the text, meditating on the text, and exegeting the text) explains the meaning of the text and applies it to their existential context. Then the transformed people of God respond in worship. Besides the Josian and Nehemian reformations, the authentic faith community is always reformed and rejuvenated whenever God's text is faithfully heard, exegeted, preached, and applied.[66]

This picture in Nehemiah 8 also introduces the practice of developing *"targumim"* as instructive, interpretive commentary on the Scriptures. The habit of the faith community at public gatherings during the Babylonian exile was to read the text of the Scriptures at synagogue in Hebrew, and then to give a paraphrase and an application of the text in Aramaic (the language of their contemporary culture). These renderings were also written down.[67] Here another type of biblical, exegetically-based, expository sermon can be seen as a vital part of the life of the faith community.

6. The Christ and the Apostles

Before Jesus is revealed in the Gospels, the figure of John the Baptist appears. John (like Moses and Samuel before him) was a hybrid. He

---

66   D. M. Lloyd-Jones wrote, "Is it not clear as you take a bird's-eye view of Church history, that the decadent periods and eras in the history of the Church have always been those periods when preaching had declined? What is it that always heralds the dawn of a Reformation or of a Revival? It is renewed preaching." Preaching and Preachers (Nashville, TN: Hodder & Stoughton, 1971), 24.

67   The earliest extant targumic material dates from the second century BC and comes from Qumran. See "TARGUMS" New Bible Dictionary, 2nd Ed. (Leicester, UK, Inter-Varsity Press), 1164. This will be especially significant when we observe Jesus' practice of reading and preaching in synagogues.

bridged two epochs. He was the last Old Testament-style prophet and the first New Testament-style evangelist. His role was that of a spokesperson, but he also heralded the introduction to the Gospel message of the coming Kingdom. It is recorded that the content of John's preaching was associated with exposition of the texts of Gen. 1:1 "the beginning," Exod. 23:20 "I will send my messenger ahead of you," Mal. 3:1 "who will prepare your way," and Isa. 40:3 "a voice of one calling in the desert" (Matt. 3:1-3). Even his diet and clothing were an application of understood texts (2 Kings 1:8, Zech. 13:4, Lev. 11:22). John demonstrated that he was a true prophet as he exegeted and applied the texts of God's written Word.

Jesus himself is unknown apart from the testimony of the Apostles, but Jesus' own ministry of preaching will be observed first, and then that of the Apostles separately. Jesus is the Word in the flesh (John 1:14). He "is the visible expression of the invisible God" (Col. 1:15 Phillips). He is not the reduction or the summary of the Word. He is the fulfillment (the fully filling reality) of the Word. He is the Prophet, the Priest, the New Adam, the Lawgiver, the King, the Messiah, the Judge, the Redeemer, the New Exodus, and the New Exile. He is the Elect, the Son of Man, and the Son of God. The focus of all revelation comes in him. Jesus Christ is like a prism through which all the centrally radiating light of God's revelation is refracted and seen.

It is recorded that "Jesus went throughout Galilee, teaching in their synagogues, preaching the good news of the kingdom, and healing every disease and sickness among the people" (Matt. 4:23 NIV). The pattern for synagogue "teaching" at this time would be for a text of the Scriptures to be read aloud in the assembly on the Sabbath. Then, following the reading, someone (sometimes the reader) would stand up before the congregation and give their interpretation (exposition) of what was read. This would be the sermon for the formative teaching and training of the people.

There is no reason to think that Jesus did not follow this practice in his synagogue proclamation. In fact, it was his custom to go to synagogue on the Sabbath (Luke 4:16). In this Lukan passage, Jesus is clearly seen following the regular custom of reading, exposition, and application of Scripture. First he read it:

> He taught in their synagogues, and everyone praised him. He went to Nazareth, where he had been brought up, and on the Sabbath day he went into the synagogue, as was his custom. And he stood up to read. The scroll of the prophet Isaiah was handed to him. Unrolling it, he found the place where it is written: "The Spirit of the Lord is on me" (Luke 4:15–18a).

Then he expounded it:

> Then he rolled up the scroll, gave it back to the attendant and sat down. The eyes of everyone in the synagogue were fastened on him, and he began by saying to them, "Today this Scripture is fulfilled in your hearing.…"

Jesus said to them, "Surely you will quote this proverb to me: 'Physician, heal yourself! Do here in your hometown what we have heard that you did in Capernaum.'"

"I tell you the truth," he continued, "no prophet is accepted in his hometown. I assure you that there were many widows in Israel in Elijah's time, when the sky was shut for three and a half years and there was a severe famine throughout the land. Yet Elijah was not sent to any of them, but to a widow in Zarephath in the region of Sidon. And there were many in Israel with leprosy in the time of Elisha the prophet, yet not one of them was cleansed—only Naaman the Syrian" (Luke 4:20–27 NIV).

Jesus takes God's Word, recorded in Isaiah 42, and reads it aloud. Though he is the proto-author of the text, he gives precedence to the text itself and defers to it for the authority and context of his message. He preaches the Word. He does not begin with himself. He reads the text, demonstrates his exegesis of it, understanding and proclaiming it to his gathered audience in their language, history, and culture. He quotes several supporting passages and applies it to their existential reality. Here Jesus is clearly demonstrating his adherence to the vital work of Spiritual formation through expositional preaching.

The congregational leaders hated him for his application of the text to himself. This shows how the Scriptures were held in such high esteem. But the people saw how his message had authority (Luke 4:32). This authority was derived from his miracles and his person, as well as his faithfulness to the prior revelation of God's written Word. Jesus exposed the meaning and significance of the scriptural Word of God throughout his ministry, quoting it, reading it, exegeting it, expositionally preaching it, teaching it, applying it, and proclaiming it.

Earl Palmer makes a case for the fact that what Jesus is doing in the Sermon on the Mount (Matt. 5–7) is what every rabbi was expected to do, in giving his expository commentary on the Law.[68] Another time that Jesus is seen appealing to the authority of the written Word of God is during his temptation by Satan in the wilderness. Satan is presented as twisting texts of Scripture to tempt Jesus to disobey his Father. Jesus refutes each text with a superior exegesis of these texts and an application of more texts. Jesus demonstrates that the only message for truth is found in the recorded written Word of God. Jesus said, "By myself I can do nothing; I judge only as I hear, and my judgment is just, for I seek not to please myself but him who sent me" (John 5:30 NIV). Even Jesus first listened to and then proclaimed the Word of God.

Lastly, Jesus is observed walking with the two disciples on the road to Emmaus. Disguised as a stranger, Jesus teaches them about the presence of "the Christ" throughout the Old Testament, through an exegetical study of the whole Scriptures.

> He said to them, "How foolish you are, and how
> slow of heart to believe all that the prophets have

---

68   See Earl Palmer, The Enormous Exception: A Commentary on the Sermon on the Mount (Waco, TX: Word Books Publishers, 1986).

spoken! Did not the Christ have to suffer these things and then enter his glory?" And beginning with Moses and all the Prophets, he explained to them what was said in all the Scriptures concerning himself (Luke 24:25–27 NIV).

That expository sermon has not been recorded for the Church. One is left, with the help of the Holy Spirit, to exegete the Scriptures in every contemporary language, history, and culture, seeing that the meaning and message of God's Word is "explained" to a new generation afresh, and that what is "said in all the Scriptures concerning [Jesus]" is proclaimed.

Finally, the Apostles represent the final witnesses of God's accumulative revelation in Jesus Christ. Jesus was the Word of God in the flesh (John 1:1–18). He is the fulfillment of all the Old Testament means of God's revelation to man. He called the Apostles to be his sent ones, to witness his works and words, and then preach his message. They were constituted by Jesus to receive the revelation of the Word, exegete and understand the revelation of the Word, proclaim the revelation of the Word, and worship the revelation of the Word (Luke 24:36–53).

The Apostles themselves consciously understood their unique task as end-time preachers. The author of Hebrews plainly writes,

> In the past God spoke to our forefathers through the prophets at many times and in various ways, but in these last days he has spoken to us by his Son, whom he appointed heir of all things, and through whom he made the universe. The Son is the radiance of God's glory and the exact representation of his being, sustaining all things by his powerful word (Heb. 1:1–3a NIV).

God spoke in the past "through the prophets" (the Old Testament), but now ("in these last days") he has spoken through Jesus, whom the Church knows through the testimony of the

Apostles (the New Testament). As the Gospel of Jesus Christ was revealed to be the new law of the new covenant, the Apostles were the new prophets who were God's designated spokesmen to form the new covenant community through applying this new law to the everyday life of the community of God. Through their preaching and teaching (recorded in their epistles) the Church was Spiritually formed. Later, like the Old Testament wisdom literature, the whole of the Scriptures is summed up in a new work of poetry and song in John's "Revelation." The Apostles, like the prophets, were not to speak on their own authority (Matt. 23:8, 1 Thess. 4:9, 1 John 2:20–27). The Apostles, like Jesus and the prophets, also demonstrated their authority to speak revelation directly from the throne of God by providing miraculous signs as proof of authentic authority.

The Apostle Paul is especially self-conscious of his commission as God's uniquely designated spokesman. He is conscious of his authority as an Apostle to declare his writings as formative Word of God (1 Cor. 2:6–13; 4:1–3, 6-7; Gal. 1:6–9; Eph. 1:9; 2:19–20; 3:4–5; Col. 1:25–29; 2 Tim. 3:10–17). The Apostle Peter declares Paul's writings as "Scripture" (2 Pet. 3:15–16). He also claims this authority for himself and his own formative teaching (2 Pet. 1:12–21).

Paul Barnett makes a convincing case that the tradition of accepting the New Testament writings of the Apostles and their contemporaries as Scripture (the Word of God on equally authoritative footing with the received canon text of the Old Testament) was well established within the lifetimes of the Apostles and within fifteen years of Jesus' death. During the apostolic age, there was a mix of both oral and written Word of God, which was the live preaching of the Apostles and the written record of their sermons.

> These texts were from the beginning self-consciously Sacred Scripture. Because they belong to the apostolic age and enjoyed the endorsement of the apostles they were always regarded as "Scripture" and located within the Canon ("yardstick"). Shorter written texts (Luke 1:1) and oral "proclamation" and "pattern of teaching" have now been gathered

up for us in the written and canonically recognized texts of the NT. The chief work of the "pastoral ministry" is to read, teach and apply the Scriptures of the OT and NT to the congregation.[69]

Paul also instructed his apprentice, Timothy, to carry on this ministry of formative preaching (2 Tim. 4:1–5). Timothy was instructed to guard the preaching of Paul (2 Tim. 1:14) and to preach Paul's preaching to reliable people who would faithfully preach it to others (2 Tim. 2:2). He was instructed to "cut straight the Word of truth"[70] (2 Tim. 2:15), that is, to carefully exegete the texts of the Scriptures. He was to be disciplined in never deviating from the received Word of God like a good soldier, a competitive athlete, and a hard-working farmer (2 Tim. 3–7). Paul considered anything less "godless chatter" (2 Tim. 2:16). As a Christian leader, Timothy was not to expect to personally receive new revelation from God. He was to pay attention to God's Word recorded in the biblical text (including Paul's and the other Apostles' writings), and he was to concentrate on his highest goal as a Spiritual leader: to set an example to his congregation by reading, preaching, and teaching the text of Scripture.

> Command and teach these things.... but set an example for the believers ... devote yourself to the public reading of Scripture, to preaching and to teaching.... Watch your life and doctrine closely. Persevere in them, because if you do, you will save both yourself and your hearers (1 Tim. 4:11–16 NIV).

The Apostles exegeted the living Word, Jesus. They observed him, listened to him, and asked him critical questions. When the

---

69   Paul Barnett, The Lost Art of Preaching, Regent College course, Vancouver, BC, 1999.
70   The Greek phrase orthotoumounta ton logon tays alaytheias can be literally translated as straight (ortho) cut (toumounta) the word (ton logon) the truth (tays alaytheias).

Holy Spirit came upon them, he gave them understanding of the Word (Jesus and the Old Testament) so that they understood the Word and proclaimed it clearly and boldly. The apostolic Gospel preaching was the exegesis and exposition of the words and works of Jesus (the text of the Word in the flesh). They also exegeted Old Testament texts, exposing God's meaning to their contemporary contexts in their language, culture, and history. This is the main way they did the work of Spiritual formation.

One example of the Apostle Paul doing exegetically-based, expository preaching is in Acts 13:14–43. In this passage, Paul was in the synagogue on the Sabbath day (Saturday), and the specific text of the Word of God (from the Law and the Prophets) for that day (as it was systematically read each week) was read aloud. The synagogue rulers asked Paul and his companions if they had a "message of encouragement [a sermon] for the people" (Acts 13:15 NIV). Paul then stood up and preached. His message was not a random, topical speech. It was an exposition of the text just read. He expounded upon the recorded text of the Word. He knew the text. He exegeted its meaning. He listened to it read out loud with the gathered congregation. He then proclaimed the meaning of the text of God's Word to the gathered faith community.

Paul makes it quite clear that the preaching ministry of a Christian leader is the primary task for the Spiritual formation of the church community. In Ephesians 4, he shows how God initiated in giving the Church the gifts and means of his revelation in a specific order. Paul writes,

> It was he who gave some to be apostles, some to be prophets, some to be evangelists, and some to be pastors and teachers, to prepare God's people for works of service, so that the body of Christ may be built up until we all reach unity in the faith and in the knowledge of the Son of God and become mature, attaining to the whole measure of the fullness of Christ (Eph. 4:11–13 NIV).

The order is unmistakable: first God initiates through his "Apostles" (Jesus' sent ones) who spoke God's Word, then "prophets" (preachers) who exegete and expound that Word to the covenant community, then "evangelists" who proclaim that Word to the lost, then "pastors" who apply that Word in shepherding the flock of God, and "teachers" who explain the basic doctrines of that Word to their flock. The purpose of all of this is that through the hearing of God's Word (read sung, prayed, and preached) the covenant people of God are "built up," reaching "unity in the faith," growing in "knowledge of the Son of God," and becoming "mature." This is authentic Spiritual formation.

The high call of Christian leadership is to find one's place in listening to and passing on God's Word so that Christians will all grow in works of service and corporate character. In 1 Timothy 3, Paul writes that if anyone wants to be a Christian leader "he must ... be able to teach" (1 Tim. 3:1-2). The job of the Christian preacher is to exegete God's revealed texts and expose the message of that revelation to his contemporary audience. Doing this properly will involve a serious effort to understand the meaning of the texts of God's Word,[71] as well as a serious effort to understand the culture and language of the listening audience to whom the preacher must expose God's revelation plainly. Understanding God's Word has always involved a careful observing of God's action, listening to him speak, asking critical questions of the Word, understanding him through Holy Spirit illumination, and proclaiming it clearly and boldly. In his seminal work on the history of Christian proclamation, Edwin C. Dargan demonstrates that this is what the early Church Fathers continued to do as faithful imitators of the Apostles.[72]

---

71 Eugene Peterson writes, "I want to pull the Christian Scriptures back from the margins of the contemporary imagination, where they have been so rudely elbowed, and reestablish them at the centre as the text for living the Christian life deeply and well.... I want to confront and expose this replacement of the authoritative Bible with the authoritative self. I want to place personal experience under the authority of the Bible and not over it. I want to set the Bible before you as the text by which we live our lives." Eat This Book: The Holy Community at Table with Holy Scripture (Vancouver, BC: Regent College Publishing, 2000).

72 Edwin C. Dargan, A History of Preaching Baker Book House, Grand Rapids, MI, 1968) p. 39

God appointed patriarchs, the lawgiver, judges, prophets, wise ones, and Apostles to first hear and then preach his Word. This Word is recorded for the Spiritual formation of the faith community. These are the "lightning, rumblings and peals of thunder" that burst from the throne of God. The Holy Christian Scriptures clarify God's general revelation through creation, point to God's specific revelation in history, and ultimately his incarnation in the life, death, and resurrection of Jesus Christ.

As an Apostle, John shows how this revelation is engaged:

> Then I saw in the right hand of him who sat on the throne a scroll with writing on both sides and sealed with seven seals. And I saw a mighty angel proclaiming in a loud voice, "Who is worthy to break the seals and open the scroll?" But no one in heaven or on earth or under the earth could open the scroll or even look inside it. I wept and wept because no one was found who was worthy to open the scroll or look inside. Then one of the elders said to me, "Do not weep! See, the Lion of the tribe of Judah, the Root of David, has triumphed. He is able to open the scroll and its seven seals...." And they sang a new song: "You are worthy to take the scroll and to open its seals, because you were slain, and with your blood you purchased men for God from every tribe and language and people and nation. You have made them to be a kingdom and priests to serve our God, and they will reign on the earth" (Rev. 4:6, 4:9–5:10 NIV).

How is this revelation perceived and received? By receiving the written Word of God (the scroll 5:1), revealed by Jesus (the Lion of Judah and the slaughtered lamb 5:5–6), exegeting it (paying careful attention to what it actually says and means), and preaching it (proclaiming that original meaning to the contemporary community context, in their language, history, and culture). This is what John was doing in Revelation. He is exegeting the whole of the written Word and teaching it to his flock in a new contextualized language.[73] He is listening to the text of God's Word and preaching it to God's people under his care.

It is only by the revelation of God himself that the Word is revealed. The Word is the self-initiated speech of God. The Word goes out in God's perfect breathing revelation to the world (the number seven is the number of perfection in apocalyptic poetry). The Church's response is to listen, receive, understand, worship, and proclaim. He has made the Church his community of kings and priests in the world, and the way the Church reigns and presides is by leading people to pay attention to God's Word read, sung, prayed, and preached. This is like the voices of the many messengers[74] (Rev. 5:11),

> numbering thousands upon thousands, and ten thousand times ten thousand. [We] encircled the throne and the living creatures and the elders. In a loud voice [we sing]: "Worthy is the Lamb, who was slain, to receive power and wealth and wisdom and strength and honor and glory and praise" (Rev. 5:11–12 NIV).

The *logos* of Christian Spiritual formation is the exposed Word of God. Authentic Christian preaching of the Word of God will always and only be, in every generation, the act of God's representative messenger, paying attention to the texts of God's Word and then boldly proclaiming the meaning of God's Word to his contemporary cultural context. Only then will the congregation truly hear the voice of God, be transformed, and then God will be glorified. This has always been the case. This has always been the true practice of

---

73 Eugene Peterson points out that John practically reworks the entire Old Testament and all of the essential themes of the New Testament into his revealing of God's Word in his apocalyptic poem, "Revelation." Reversed Thunder (San Francisco, CA: HarperCollins Publishers, 1988), 23.
74 The word aggelos literally means messenger.

the authentic covenant people of God, whether in the tabernacle or the temple, in synagogues or sanctuaries, churches or cathedrals.[75]

> Then I heard every creature in heaven and on earth and under the earth and on the sea, and all that is in them, singing: "To him who sits on the throne and to the Lamb be praise and honor and glory and power, for ever and ever!" The four living creatures said, "Amen," and the elders fell down and worshiped (Rev. 5:13–14 NIV).

This is a beautiful picture of "God's throne," given through John's Scripture-soaked imagination, his love for God, his skill with words, and his love for his parishioners, to whom he writes by the inspiration of the Holy Spirit. What he gives them is a picture of "what is to happen"—the invisible reality of God being adored by his people through the "open door" of worship. God is revealed in concentric circles. Beginning with the rainbow and jewel-lit throne, God's person radiates out through the four living creatures (his creation), the elders (his prophets and Apostles), and the angels (his revealing message). The "Lion of Judah" (the incarnated Christ) opens the scroll (Holy Scripture) and the sacraments (baptism in the "glassy sea" and the Lord's supper through "a Lamb … who had been slain") amongst the seven lamp stands (God's people assembled in church communities).

Here the action of worship is revealed. This is the picture of the invisible context of the Church at worship. In the midst of feeble attempts at serving God, his people are caught up in the world-shaking events of God's eternal throne room. In the public reading, praying, preaching, singing, and sacraments, God's people are involved in the heavenly drama of this cosmic transformation, whether they realize it or not. In the midst of weekly Sunday church

---

75   John Stott provides an excellent, yet brief, history of "expository preaching" throughout the Christian era, giving examples of faithful "preachers" from over two thousand centuries who represented what we have here described as "authentic Christian preaching" (The Glory of Preaching: A Historical Sketch in Between Two Worlds, 15–47).

service, the elders fall on their faces and lay their crowns before the throne. All of creation sees and proclaims his glory. The thunder and lightning of his revelation come from the center of his throne. The creatures, elders, and angels all sing his praise, which culminates in the triumphal "Amen!"

The essence of authentic Christian Spiritual formation through preaching can be seen throughout the panorama of the entire story of God's redemptive history, recorded in the Scriptures. The fundamental task of the Spiritual leader has always and only been to listen to God's Word, understand God's meaning, and proclaim it to his contemporary community. The Christian leader is to lead his people to pay attention to God. In these last days, God is paid attention to through the text of his spoken Word, the Bible (Heb. 1:1–3). The primary call of the Christian leader, then, is to continue to exegete God's Word and teach it to his community. John Stott points out that when the Church has neglected to execute its first duty to authentic, exegetically-based, expository preaching, it has experienced its eras of decline and weakness in strength, numbers, and vitality.[76]

Imagine I had to suddenly leave my home for a foreign country without saying good-bye to my family. But, before I left, I dictated a letter for my family to a friend and charged him with the task of delivering my message to my family. Suppose, though, on the way to deliver this message to my family, my friend decided that what my family really needed to hear was a series of lectures on his opinions of the perfect family. He then delivered these lectures, using quotes from my letter, taken out of context, to back up his points. If I found out he had done this, I would be furious at my friend! I gave him a message for my family. His task was to deliver it to them with no embellishments or distractions. I would say, "Just deliver the message! Only add what you need to say to help them

---

76 Stott writes, "It is clear … that God hinged the welfare of his people on their listening to his voice, believing his promises and obeying his commands." He then quotes E. C. Dargan and G. H. Doran (History of Preaching Vol. 1 A.D. 70–1572, London, UK: Hodder & Stoughton, 1905), "Decline of Spiritual life and activity in the churches is commonly accompanied by a lifeless, formal, unfruitful preaching" (Between Two Worlds, 114).

understand it because they weren't there when I dictated it!" I believe God is furious over what passes for preaching in many churches. He has given a message to his family and has appointed teachers and preachers to "just deliver the message!" and to only add what they need to add to help God's family understand it because they are in a new context. His message is his transformative Word. It is to be listened to, understood, and obeyed. This is the fundamental task of Christian attention.

Some may assert, "Of course the content of Christian proclamation is the Scriptures. That's obvious." If it is obvious, why is it so often not practiced? Why do we find, in so many gatherings of God's people, that there is so much topical human opinion being proclaimed, while God's plain message to His family is ignored or changed? The fundamental task of making sure God's Word is heard is not just the responsibility of Christian leaders. The people of God must take responsibility for their own Spiritual formation. They must demand that their leaders lead them to the authentic center, giving them a hearing of God's authentic Word. The following is called "The Job Description of the Congregation," and it addresses what the congregation should do to their Christian leader:

> Fling him into his office, tear the office sign from the door and nail on the sign "study." Take him off all mailing lists. Lock him up with his books, his typewriter, and his Bible. Slam him down on his knees before texts and broken hearts and the flick of lives of a superficial flock and a holy God. Force him to be the one man in our surfeited communities who knows about God. Throw him into the ring to box with God until he learns how short his arms are. Engage him to wrestle with God all the night through. And let him come out only when he is bruised and beaten into being a blessing. Shut his mouth forever spouting remarks and stop his tongue forever tripping lightly over every nonessential. Require him to have something to say before he

dares break the silence, and bend his knees in the lonesome valley of prayer. Burn his eyes with weary study. Wreck his emotional poise with worry for God. And make him exchange his pious stance for a humble walk with God and man. Make him spend and be spent for the glory of God. Rip out his telephone. Burn up his ecclesiastical records. Put water in his fuel tank. Give him a Bible, tie him to the pulpit, and make him preach the Word of the living God. Test him, quiz him, examine him, humiliate him for his ignorance of things divine. Shame him for his good comprehension of finances, game scores, and politics. Laugh at his frustrated effort to play psychiatrist. Form a choir, raise a chant, and haunt him with it night and day "Sir, we would see Jesus." When at long last, he dares assay the pulpit, ask him if he has a word from God. If he doesn't, dismiss him. Tell him you can read the morning paper and digest the television commentaries and think through the day's superficial problems and manage the community's weary drives and bless the sordid baked potatoes, green beans ad infinitum, better than he can. Command him not to come back until he's read and re-read, written and re-written until he can stand up worn, and forlorn, and say, "Thus saith the Lord." Break him across the board of his ill-gotten popularity. Smack him hard with his own prestige. Corner him with questions about God. Cover him with demands for celestial wisdom. And give him no escape until he's back against the wall of the word. And sit down before him and listen to the only word he has left: God's Word. Let him be totally ignorant of the down street gossip. But give him a chapter and order him to walk around it, camp on it, sup with it, and come at last to speak it backward and forward, until he says about it all things that ring with the truth of eternity. And when he's burned up by the flaming word, when he's consumed at last by the fiery grace blazing through him, and when he's privileged to translate the truth of God to men, and finally transferred from earth to heaven, then bear him away gently and blow a muted trumpet and lay down softly, place a two-edged sword on his coffin, and raise the tune triumphant. For he was a brave soldier of the Word and ere he died he had become a man of God.[77]

---

77   From "And Preach As You Go" by Floyd Doud Shafer published in Christianity Today March 27, 1961. Used with permission.

Chapter 3
The Context of Spiritual Formation

The Cultural Shift

There may be an impending crisis for the future of the evangelical Church in the West. The Western Church is grappling with the effects of the major cultural shift in popular culture from a modernist worldview to a postmodern one. The term "postmodern" is used here to indicate the contemporary worldview in the West, which has arisen in the collapse of the "modern" worldview since the mid-twentieth century. As contemporary pastors, congregations, and denominations grapple with the radical impacts of postmodernism on Western culture, a new generation of pastors is reinventing church life and practice. This reinvention may include a growing abandonment of the exposition of the Scriptures as a central aspect of Spiritual formation. Roy Clements writes, "Evidence is mounting of a growing disillusionment with expository preaching."[78] David Hilborn claims that expository preaching was merely a product of the modernist Enlightenment age. He writes of several "contemporary

---

78   Roy Clements, "Expository Preaching in a Post Modern World," Cambridge Papers vol. 7, no. 3 (September 1998), 174.

evangelical leaders who are convinced the expository age is coming to an end." [79]

One young Christian leader told me, "I hate preaching."[80] He went on to say that he especially hates the performance that typically takes place in his churchgoing experience, wherein a pastor gets in front of his congregation, puts on his "preaching voice," and prattles on about "religious" ideas that have little to do with the "real world" where we passionately live. This leader loves God, and he desires to personally know the Lord and his will. But he is voicing a common sentiment towards what the word "preaching" has come to mean in the postmodern age.

In contemporary Western culture, the word "preaching" can have the reputation of being long, boring, and rationalistic. Doug Pagitt calls this modernist style of preaching "speaching."[81] Contemporary church leaders are engaging a culture that sees little value in listening to the Scriptures presented in this manner. Hadden Robinson's book *Expository Preaching* is being used today as the textbook for teaching authentic church practice "in 120 seminaries and Bible Colleges" and has recently been re-released for a new generation of Christians with the only real update being an exploration of "narrative preaching."[82] There is an apparent disconnect between what church leaders are being taught as important in 120 seminaries in America and what is being perceived as important in these postmodern emergent churches.

Dan Kimball states, "Even people's view of preachers has changed. What once was a respectable role in society is now unfavorably stereotyped. Even the word, preach, is now a negative one."[83] John Stott, lamenting the decline of expository preaching, observes that in the late twentieth century, the "tide of preaching ebbed, and the ebb is still low today. At least in the western world the decline of

---

79   David Hilborn, Picking up the Pieces (Nashville, TN: Hodder & Stoughton, 1997), 5.

80   From a conversation with me in 1999.

81   Doug Pagitt, Preaching Re-Imagined: The Role of the Sermon in Communities of Faith (Grand Rapids, MI: Zondervan, 2005). 48

82   Interview with Hadden Robinson, Preaching Magazine (July/August 2001).

83   Dan Kimball, The Emerging Church (Grand Rapids, MI: Zondervan, 2003), 173.

preaching is a symptom of the decline of the Church."[84] Later he writes, "The prophets of doom in today's Church are confidently predicting that the day of preaching is over. It is a dying art, they say, an outmoded form of communication, an echo from an abandoned past."[85] Stott, along with many others, would argue that there is a fundamental approach to receiving and transmitting God's Word, which is the essence of authentic Christian Spiritual formation and which transcends any generational context. The instructive Word of God has been the essential instrument of individual and corporate Spiritual formation for the entire history of the faith community of God. But, in this postmodern age, "instruction" itself is in disrepute.

Biblical preaching has had a central role in the life of the Evangelical Church for centuries. During the modernist era, however, the sermon may have taken on some of the enculturation of the times, often being rationalistic, deductive, lecture-oriented, propositional, authoritarian, and analytical. For some, the notion of the "sermon" (and "evangelicalism" as well) has become synonymous with the modernist paradigm, and so, they would argue, it must be abandoned or at least so radically reoriented that it becomes something quite different.

Some would argue that this has had a detrimental effect on the life of the Church in the West. D.M. Lloyd-Jones writes, "Is it not clear as you take a bird's-eye view of Church history, that the decadent periods and eras in the history of the Church have always been those periods when preaching had declined? What is it that always heralds the dawn of a Reformation or of a Revival? It is renewed preaching."[86]

One can also see that preaching is in crisis for the contemporary Western Church when T.D. Jakes is called "America's Best Preacher"[87] on the cover of *Time* Magazine. Inside the magazine he is quoted as

---

84   John W. Stott, Between Two Worlds: The Challenge of Preaching Today (Grand Rapids, MI: William B. Eerdmans Publishing Company, 1982), 43.
85   Ibid, 50.
86   D. M. Lloyd-Jones, Preaching and Preachers (Nashville, TN: Hodder & Stoughton, 1971), 24.
87   Time Magazine (September 17, 2001).

saying, "The rules are, Get [*sic*] the message over any way you can. The more tools you have, the better it is."[88] Unfortunately, Jakes may have more "tools" than "message." The article includes a transcript of part of Jakes' sermon on Genesis 1.[89] It is encouraging that he uses a biblical text. But one can quickly see that he misuses the actual text to teach his own ideas of self-awareness and self-actualization, and even his own version of modalist heresy.[90]

Is Jakes any kind of authentic model for Christian preaching? His passion is evident. He seems to be touching a popular nerve in his particular audience. But, if he is teaching modalism and eisogeting rather than exegeting the Scriptures, it can be argued that he is not actually communicating God's Word. Meanwhile, 23 percent of responding subscribers of *Leadership Weekly* voted Jakes (tied with Chuck Swindoll) as "the number one effective preacher today."[91] One must ask, "effective" at what? The vital question that needs to be asked of any Christian leader, in any culture, in every generation, is, does he effectively expose his people to the true Word of God?

The Context of Postmodernism

To understand the issues of the Western postmodern paradigm, one must see it in its juxtaposition with Western modernism. Likewise, Western modernism itself can only be understood in its contrast and reaction to Western premodernism. Finally, all these patterns must be contrasted with the biblical paradigm. Figure 7 is a chart showing the differences between each of these paradigms when contrasted with each other in their approach to nine seminal issues.[92]

---

88   Ibid, 62.
89   Ibid, 63.
90   In an in-depth evaluation of T. D. Jakes' teachings, the Christian Research Journal (vol. 22, no. 2) exposes this popular teacher as a modalist, while Christianity Today (Feb. 7, 2000) bemoans his pop-psychology version of faith.
91   Leadership Journal (Winter 2002).
92   Contents of this chart were adapted from a similar chart first presented to me at a seminar on postmodernism in 1998. The seminar presenter does not know the origins of the original chart. I have adapted and expanded the original chart.

The first thing to consider is the "worldview." This is the overarching way of seeing the world, which dominates the imagination of culture. The second consideration is what constitutes the "final authority" for each era in question. This is the issue of how truth is understood and mitigated. The third thing to consider is the issue of what people see their "life governed by." This is the issue of how social structure is ordered. The fourth consideration is the "place of God" in the social structure of each given era.[93]

figure 7[94]

ISSUES	BIBLICAL	PREMODERN	MODERN	POSTMODERN
Worldview	Theistic	Superstitious	Secular / Naturalistic	Pluralistic
Final Authority	Christ in the Scriptures	Church / Monarch	Reason	Feelings
Life Governed by	Theology	Fear	Principals	Personal Preference
Place of God	Over All	Distant Ruler	Distant / Absent	Replaced by spiritualities
Place of Self	Under God	Within Feudal Hierarchy	At the Centre Under No One	Unanchored / Responsible to No One
Place of Others	There for Self to Serve	Competition	For Mutual Benefit	There for Self to Use
Place of Creation	To be Cared For	Equal to Self	Under the Self	Over the Self
Morality Governed by	Virtue	Law	Ethics	Personal Choice
Life Lived for	The Glory of God	The Glory of Rulers	The Glory of Man	Whatever

The fifth thing to consider is the "place of the self." This is the question of where the individual fits within the structure of society. Sixth is the consideration of the "place of others." This is the question of how individuals relate to other individuals and to the larger community. The seventh consideration is the issue of the "place of creation" in the governing of life in each era. Creation would consist of everything in the natural world besides humans and their

93   For a discussion of the role of imagination in the construction of theology, see Garrett Green, Imagining God: Theology and the Religious Imagination (San Francisco, CA: Harper and Row, 1989).
94   This chart has been revised and expanded from material I acquired through a seminar on postmodernism. The seminar leader did not know the source of the original material on which this chart is based.

social and technological structures. Eighth is the question of what "morality is governed by" in each era. This is the way that the rules of social interaction are understood and regulated. The ninth and final consideration is what "life is lived for." This is how the purpose of life is understood and followed.

The Biblical Worldview

One must consider each of these issues in light of biblical Christianity. First, the biblical worldview is a theistic one. One must begin with God at the center. He is radiating out from the center his revelation of his character and will to his whole creation.[95] This is the overarching imagination of the biblical Christian perspective. God is preeminent in all things. Everything fits together into his plan for life and faith.

Final authority in all matters of life and faith, then, is God. But the Church must be more specific and say that all final authority is in Christ, who is the visible revelation of the invisible God (Col. 1:15). God has given him all authority in heaven and earth (Matt. 28:18). Here the Church must be even more specific, for neither Christ nor his authority is known apart from his revelation, which is recorded for us in the Scriptures. These must all be put together for a proper biblical perspective. Final authority rests in Christ, revealed through the canon of the Holy Christian Scriptures. These Scriptures must be the arbitrator for teaching, correcting, rebuking, and training (2 Tim. 3:16–17).

Next, it must be noted that life is governed by theology. Theology must be understood as "God (*theos*) understanding (*logos*)" rather than merely the ideas and philosophies of theologians, preachers, or religious leaders. How is "God understanding" gained? God has revealed everything his people need to know for life and faith in the Scriptures. Therefore, the Word of God must be studied to understand his character and will. This "God understanding"

---

95   See Chapter 2: Theological Reflection.

is proper theology, and it must guide all Christian thinking and living.

Following this, the place of God must be seen as supreme in all Christian thinking and living. He is at the center, not any individual or philosophy. Christians recognize him in both individual and collective imagination as the center of all things. It follows, then, that the place of self (personal opinions and feelings) is under God and peripheral to his revealed truth. The human cries of "Who am I?" or "Where do I fit in?" are only answered as one finds one's place in the periphery of God's being.

As the place of God and the self is understood in light of biblical revelation, the place of others and of creation follows. The place of others is that others are there for the self to serve (Matt. 20:25–28). Christians are to relate to one another in light of God's generosity to us. He has freely given. Believers can freely give. He has freely forgiven. His followers can freely forgive. He freely serves. Christians can freely serve. Likewise, it is understood from God's revelation that all of creation is his, and humans are here as caregivers.

In the biblical Christian paradigm, morality is governed by virtue. Morality is something God does by his Holy Spirit in and through individuals. They are not under religious law. They do not perform good deeds for God. Their best efforts are as filthy rags to him. Rather, his Holy Spirit resides with Christian believers, and he produces his fruit in them and through them (Gal. 5:22–23). His Law is written on their hearts. Finally, in the biblical paradigm, life is lived for the glory of God. He alone is sovereign. All things are by him, with him, in him, and for him.

The Premodern Worldview

The worldview of Western premodernism (before the seventeenth century and the Enlightenment) was dominated by superstition. The overarching popular imagination of the premodern person was one filled with ideas of supernatural causes for natural events. Meaning was understood through tradition and myth.[96] The Constantinian age ushered in state support for the Church. The Church had later become institutionalized in the Holy Roman Empire. In this feudal world, with hundreds of European kingdoms vying for wealth, resources, and dominance, the final authority for life and faith was the Church, represented by the reigning monarch.[97] Truth was officiated through the governance of church and state leaders. Papal decrees and kingly edicts were instantly and unquestioningly understood as supreme law. This was a time of the assumed divine right of kings to rule their servile people. Life was governed by fear-filled obedience to the reigning leadership. Order was kept through the rule of the state and church law.

The place of God was understood in relation to the place of authority in the cultural context. Just as authority rested in the supremacy of distant church and state supreme leaders, so the imagined place of God was as a distant supreme being. Likewise, the place of the self was seen as fitting within the feudal hierarchy. One knew one's place as each individual held a static station from church and state royalty down to the landless peasant class. The place of others was seen in terms of their place in the overall social competition for survival as cities and states vied for control of precious resources.

The place of creation in the premodern mindset was on equal par with the self and others in the seasonal struggle for survival. People competed with animals, disease, and even weather for survival. Morality was governed by the power of the ruler of the day through his rule of law. And the whole of premodern life was lived by individuals and their communities for the glory of sovereign human rulers and their state and religious institutions.

---

96   Ronald J. Allen, "As the Worldviews Turn: Six Key Issues for Preaching in a Postmodern Ethos" in Encounter, Winter 1996.
97   David Buttrick, "Speaking Between the Times: Homiletics in a Postmodern World in Theology and the Interhuman" in Robert R. Williams (ed.), Theology and the Interhuman: Essays In Honor of Edward Farley (Valley Forge, PA: Trinity Press International, 1995), 147.

The Modern Worldview

One can see that the two-hundred-year-old experiment of Western modernism (roughly from the mid-eighteenth century through the mid-twentieth century)[98] is in every way a reaction to what was Western premodernism. During the age of liberation and the development of individualism in Europe, a revolutionary new "Enlightenment" in thought and practice transformed Western civilization. With the rise of scientific discovery, new educational initiatives, world exploration, technological inventions, and medical advancements, a profound optimism gripped the West.[99] This created a radically new worldview. Writers such as David Hume in England and Immanuel Kant in Germany published works that challenged the status quo and began to influence the popular Western imagination.[100]

No longer was the West a prisoner to superstition. Secular natural explanations for all of life's experiences were being discovered and hypothesized. With the rise of individualism, rational thought replaced corrupt monarchs and Church despots as the final authority. No longer did an individual have to languish under the autocratic rule of tyrannical rule. Every individual could question "truth" as it had been handed down to him or her by government and religious institutions.[101]

No longer did life have to be governed by fear. Rather, rational thought replaced institutional superstitious ideas with reasonable principles. One could reason out an individual's rights, freedoms, and responsibilities based on the scientific method. Individuals were now democratically free to design for themselves a personal interpretation of truth for life and faith. The most popular form

---

98   Though modern ideas were being published in philosophy and the arts well before 1750 (i.e. Francis Bacon was writing modernist ideas 150 years before Kant), it takes many years for academic ideas to be accepted and applied to popular life and faith.
99   Henderson, 99.
100   Kant's Critique of Pure Reason (1781) was one of the most influential modernist philosophical works since the Middle Ages, establishing modernism as the force for the "enlightenment" of a new age.
101   Buttrick, "Speaking Between the Times," 146.

of entertainment in Western Europe and America became rational debates between famous orators.[102]

The place of God, therefore, was seen not only as distant, but also as absent.[103] All moral questions of life and faith could be answered through the application of biblical principles, in the same way as all physical problems could be answered through the application of scientific principles. In a sense, a living God was no longer needed. He could be replaced by a rational deism.

The place of self in the modern paradigm was no longer seen as under the right of church and state rulers. Rather, it was seen as at the center, under no one. Each individual self was his own authority, possessing his own personal rights. American cultural critic George Steiner writes,

> The arbitrariness of all aesthetic propositions, of all value judgments is inherent in human consciousness and human speech. Anything can be said about anything.... A critical theory, an aesthetic, is a politics of taste.... No aesthetic proposition can be termed either "right" or "wrong." The sole appropriate response is personal assent or dissent.[104]

The place of others was seen as existing for mutual benefit. An optimism for Western government fueled European missionary zeal to bring "good government" to all people. Colonial expansion brought Western law, morality, and commerce to all areas of the planet.

The place of creation was seen as coming under the self. Nature was no longer seen as being an equal competitor with the self, but rather as a resource to be subdued, controlled, and exploited by

---

102 Neil Postman makes the point in his book, Amusing Ourselves to Death (New York, NY: Penguin Books, 1984, 33–49) that during the nineteenth century, Western culture was a print-dominated culture that craved lecture-style rational debates. He argues that during this modernist era, people thought in whole paragraphs, while today people think in sound bites.

103 Henderson, 128.

104 George Steiner, No Passion Spent (New Haven, CT: Yale University Press, 1996), 25–26.

modern people.[105] Likewise, morality was no longer governed by the irrational dictates of premodern rulers, but by ethics, derived from the rational interpretation of biblical principles. Ethical principles were imposed on people and society from the outside to control moral behavior. Finally, under the modern paradigm, all of life was lived for the glory of human progress. The human being was sovereign and all that served human enterprise was considered good and right.

Everywhere modernism judged premodernism as wrong, it was right. The superstitious nature of life in premodern Western civilization was oppressive. Individuals were often subjugated to corrupt rulers wielding unreasonable power. Natural pestilence and discomfort were a cruel experience. Modern advances in medicine, education, technology, and science have helped the entire world. Unfortunately, in reaction to the excesses of premodernism, Western civilization established modernism as a just-as-wrong alternative to biblical Christianity.

The Postmodern Worldview

Just as modernist philosophers began to question premodern assumptions long before the modernist Enlightenment took hold of Western civilization, postmodern philosophers and artists began to challenge the ideas and mores of the modernist paradigm. Near the turn of the twentieth century, Virginia Woolf wrote scandalous stories that challenged the accepted mores of human sexuality. Albert Einstein's theory of relativity challenged the accepted ideas of Newtonian science. Karl Marx challenged the rightness of Western capitalist commerce. Ideas like these took time to sink into the popular imagination.

One event, however, shattered the entrenched optimism of modernism in Western civilization more than any other. At a time when it was assumed that with enough good Western science,

---

105   Albert Borgmann, Crossing the Postmodern Divide (Chicago, IL: University of Chicago Press, 1992), Chapters 1 and 2.

education, medicine, government, and religion, modernism could conquer every problem and virtually bring heaven to earth, the two nations that had the best Western science, education, medicine, government, and religion went to war in the most horrific conflict the world had yet witnessed. Germany and England (and their allies) fought across Europe, devastating a continent and a generation. Following World War I was a global influenza pandemic, a global economic depression, and a second world war. By the 1950s, Western optimism was replaced with a new pessimism that precipitated the revolutionary postmodern paradigm shift.[106]

As modernism was in every way a reaction to premodernism, so postmodernism is in every way a reaction to modernism. Unfortunately, though, postmodernism sets up a just-as-wrong alternative to biblical revelation.

The optimistic secular worldview of modernism has been replaced with a pluralistic worldview. David Henderson writes,

> Postmodernism is a rejection of Enlightenment thinking, the rationalism and optimism of the modern world. Purpose, design, objective truth, absolutes, and any idea of overarching "metanarratives" or "totalizing discourses" are thrown out the window. Instead, postmodernism embraces the nihilism of and perspectivism of Nietzsche and the existentialism of Sartre. Life is pointless. There is no inherent meaning or purpose in life and there is no truth.[107]

The politically correct liberalism of postmodern Western civilization accepts all opinions as being pluralistically "true." The concept of "truth" itself has been deconstructed and is now popularly understood to be a perspective, and only one piece of a pluralist mosaic of opinions. Therefore, contradictory ideas can be

---

106   Buttrick, "Speaking Between the Times," 151.
107   Henderson, 192.

held to be mutually "true" in that they merely represent differing perspectives.

In the post-Einstein world, human reason was found to be an unreliable arbiter for understanding reality. Postmodernism has replaced rationalism with sentimentalism. Human experience and feelings have replaced reason as the most trustworthy final authority. If the truth about life and faith is relative, one can rely on personal experience and personal revelation to be as—or even more—authoritative than the Scriptures.

Life, then, is governed not by principles, but by personal preference. There is a post-liberal idea in postmodernism that suggests that Jesus and the Bible may be true for Christians, but not necessarily for others.[108] In the smorgasbord of religious ideas available to the Western postmodern person, the individual's personal preference is the final governance for life and faith practice. The highest form of religious freedom is the liberty of each individual to make personal choices in every area of life and faith.

The place of God in the imaginations of postmoderns has been replaced by a myriad of spiritualities. This contemporary Western generation is religiously sophisticated. It is exposed to a plethora of religious traditions and ideas, which are being picked over, accepted, and combined with pluralistic zeal to create new relativistic personal religions. John Stackhouse Jr. writes,

> When it comes to ultimate matters, then, many of our North American neighbors have resorted to a secularism that frees one from all religious authority to a hyper-individualistic "religion a la carte." Indeed, our society's tolerance of do-it-yourself religion is, itself, a manifestation of secularization.

108   John Shelby Spong is one champion of this concept. He is a bishop in the Episcopal Church in America, leading in its rituals and theological training, yet he works to undermine the universal claims of Christianity through books like The Sins of Scripture: Exposing the Bible's Texts of Hate to Reveal the God of Love (New York, NY: HarperCollins Publishers, 2005) and Rescuing the Bible from Fundamentalism : A Bishop Rethinks the Meaning of Scripture (New York, NY: HarperCollins Publishers, 1991).

> For in leaving questions of the reality of God or the
> gods up to each individual, this attitude implies that
> there really aren't any such supernatural entities.[109]

The highest value for postmoderns is tolerance. The least tolerated notion from modernism is the idea that one religious expression is better than another. It is interesting that angels, demons, ghosts, and miracles are more prevalent in popular postmodern culture than they were in the modernist context. American movies and television, capitalizing on the religious milieu of the nation and the surprising popularity of Mel Gibson's movie *The Passion of the Christ*, are addressing issues of the supernatural and religious. Meanwhile, mainline churches in North America are losing adherents at an alarming rate.[110]

The place of the self in the postmodern context is "unanchored"[111] and responsible to no one. There is a fixation with the freedom of the adolescent lifestyle in popular Western culture. Staying young, fit, and active are the highest of values, while responsibility, wisdom, and maturity are abhorred. The place of others is seen in terms of their value in serving the self. Others are there for the self to use. Relationships become a means to an end in the service of personal fulfillment. The self exploits the relationship to get what it can from the other and then discards the other when it is of no more use to the self. This is a disposable culture. Marriages, churches, friends, and business associations can all be discarded when they no longer serve the perceived needs of the self. No-fault divorce is an invention of the postmodern Western world. It is simply a symptom of a wider throwaway society.

---

109   John Stackhouse Jr., "Speaking in Tongues" in Crux (Regent College, Vancouver, BC, Vol. 25, No. 4, December 1999), 4.

110   Canadian sociologist Reginald Bibby has found that weekly church attendance in Canada fell from 31 percent of the national population in 1975, to 21 percent in 2000. The largest drop in numbers occurred in the Roman Catholic Church, especially in Quebec, followed closely by the Mainline Protestant Churches. See Reginald W. Bibby, Restless Churches: How Canada's Churches Can Contribute to the Emerging Religious Renaissance (Kelowna, BC: Wood Lake Books, 2005).

111   Faith Popcorn coined the term "unanchored" to describe this generation in The Popcorn Report (New York, NY: Doubleday Books, 1991).

However, the place of creation in the postmodern context is over the self. Nature has come to be seen as practically a deity to be served. The virtues of ecological preservation are unquestioned by the majority of postmoderns, and the literal worship of nature through pagan religions is on the rise in the West,[112] with significant representation of the "Covenant of the Goddess" at the 2004 Parliament of World Religions.[113] Meanwhile, the United Nations Environmental Protection Agency names Christianity as a source cause of environmental problems in its 1995 document *The Global Biodiversity Assessment*.[114]

In the postmodern context, morality is governed by personal choice. The popular way of judging whether something is morally acceptable is whether someone's rights are perceived to be in danger of being violated. Anything is permissible, then, as long as "no one gets hurt." Each individual defines his own morality based on his perception and interpretation of individual personal rights. It can be said that in the postmodern context, life is lived for "whatever." If there is no objective truth, and morality is governed by personal choice, then the purpose of life is determined by the sovereignty of each individual. It is no longer asked, "Is it true?" Rather, it is asked, "Do I like it?"

Much of the postmodern revolution has been seen as a threat to biblical Christianity. It must be stressed, however, that everywhere postmodernism has judged modernism to be wrong, it is right, and everywhere the Church has replaced biblical faith with modernist faith, it is wrong. Placing faith in natural science or human rationalism is idolatry. Reducing the revelation of God to "principles to live by" is flawed. Placing the self at the center of reality, independent of a distant God, over others and creation, is erroneous.

---

112   Bibby, 39.

113   Donald H. Frew, Pagans in Interfaith Dialogue: New Faiths, New Challenges (CoGWeb, http://cog.org/pwr/don.html).

114   The Global Biodiversity Assessment is a 1,100 plus page interpretation of the UN Convention on Biological Diversity. It fingered historical Christianity as a key component of environmental problems. Western-based economic concepts, industrial advances and technological breakthroughs, and Western versions of production and resource use were all linked as negative examples of the Christian religion, showing it as an adverse force on cultures, economies, and ecosystems.

The Church must not conform to the patterns of its day (Rom. 12:2); it must vigorously engage the imagination of its contemporary setting. It is a postmodern world, and the Church must engage the milieu of its environment as the missional agency of God. Premodernism, modernism, and postmodernism are all active and observable in the contemporary Christian context. One can observe a kind of active premodern faith in sectarian institutions and their superstitions in some forms of Roman Catholicism and Eastern Orthodoxy. One can observe a kind of active modernist faith in the rational, principle-based approaches of various fundamentalist and evangelical traditions. One can also observe a kind of active postmodern faith in the spiritualism found in certain experientially-based, neo-Pentecostal movements. All forms of Christian expression must be evaluated against the biblical paradigm revealed by God, while every cultural context must be engaged with the Bible's message. One can utilize what is positive about each culture's contextual paradigm and connect it to Spiritual formation through authentic contextualized preaching of the Word of God.

Lorne Wilkinson sees the rise of this new, proud, and popular philosophy in Western culture as a throwback to ancient, earthy cults, while at the same time being a hip, eco, pseudo (post-quantum physics) science-loving, postmodern, marketing-savvy religious phenomenon.[115] Wilkinson lives in Vancouver, which is the Mecca of Canadian left-coast ideologies and boasts a historically low church attendance of 2 percent of the population. In a recent survey of adolescents, 75 percent of British Columbian teenagers reported having no religious affiliation whatsoever.[116] Wilkinson is aware of these statistics and lives amongst the people who embody them. One could despair over the lack of commitment to the historic, biblical, Christian faith of a generation ago. Wilkinson, however, sees great opportunities for the Gospel to be heard in new and fresh ways. He also demonstrates, through his understanding of these throwback

---

115   Lorne Wilkinson, The Bewitching Charms of Neopaganism (Christianity Today Magazine, September 27, 2001).

116   The 1998 McCreary Report, http://www.mcs.bc.ca/rs_pprojects.htm.

ideologies, something of authentic Christian spirituality, which has been lost through Evangelicalism's ties with the modernist agenda.

Over the last four hundred years, the Western Church has identified too much with the Newtonian paradigm of the universe. The collective realization of God was lost. Wilkinson argues for a rescuing of this respect for the earth and a capitulation to the "spiritualities" of neopaganism where they have got it right. Here is common ground for introducing people to the Creator of the earth, the God of the universe. Wilkinson argues that Christians do not need to be afraid of these people. They have more to fear from us. In the past, rather than seeing where God may be revealing himself to them through his creation, Christians burned many of them at the stake.

Lesslie Newbigin's seminal book on missiology, *Foolishness to the Greeks*, discusses the matter of realizing and articulating the authentic historic Christian *kerygma*[117] in the midst of our contemporary culture. He brings his vast experience of cross-cultural evangelism to bear on examining the essential good news of the Christian faith in contrast to the culturally bound trappings of Western Christianity. From his vantage point of being a virtual stranger to Western culture after being in the foreign mission field for so long, he distinguishes between *contextualizing* the true Gospel to our Western mindset and *indiginizing* (or *adapting*) the message to that mindset.[118] He insists, with al-Ghazali (the Muslim theologian and mystic), that Christians must distinguish between the true signs of transcendence and the false ones through sober rational assessment.[119]

Newbigin argues that the authority for distinguishing between the true and the false signs of transcendence is the Christian Scriptures. He contrasts the authentic approach to the Bible from several historic popular approaches to it. He dismisses the "fundamentalist" approach to treating the Bible in a wooden literal sense. He rejects the popular Gnostic approach to the Bible where it is used as a personal spiritualist text that merely confirms one's esoteric experiences. He also spurns the use of the Bible as an encyclopedia

---

117 Kerygma means "the content of the preached message."
118 Newbigin, 2.
119 Ibid, 13.

of morality. He refuses the neo-orthodox view of the hidden, divine story-behind-the-story-of-the-Bible approach. Instead, he embraces (with Frei, Lindbeck, and others) the approach to the authority of the Bible that sees in this document of divine origin the true witness that "renders accessible to us the character and actions and purposes of God."[120]

Newbigin investigates what the true witness of the Scriptures has to offer in its dialogue with science and politics. These two pillars of modernist, secular ideology are dealt with clearly and definitively. Newbigin makes a great case for the Christian's confidence in the midst of opposing views. Here, Newbigin does what Alister McGrath commends us to do, challenging believers to "rattle their cages," rather than seeing themselves as being "in the cage getting rattled."[121]

Finally, Newbigin challenges the postmodern Church of Jesus Christ to continue to be the authentic faith community it has always been within the context of every culture, influencing our culture as agents of profound relatedness in bonds of mutual love and obedience that reflect the mutual relatedness in love that is the being of the Triune God himself. This is done, Newbigin says, by being communities of transformative truth and grace, and by being led by the Holy Spirit into all understanding. In this way, Christians can boldly engage in dialogue with science and politics (or any other ideology of any age) with confidence in the person of Jesus Christ and the knowledge of his revealed truth found in the Scriptures.

The Emergent Church

There is a growing phenomenon in Western Christianity sometimes called "The Emergent Church." This term was first coined by Brian McLaren in his essay *They Say It's Just a Phase*[122] to describe a loose

---

120   Ibid, 59.
121   Rattling the Cages was a course offered by Alaster McGrath at Regent College, Vancouver, BC, 1994.
122   Next-Wave website, October 2000, http://www.next-wave.org/Nove00/phase. htm (accessed December 12, 2000).

association of postmodern congregations being led by young neo-evangelical pastors. McLaren is described by Robert Webber as one of the leaders of this phenomenon.[123] Emergent churches are effecting monumental influence upon contemporary Christianity. One of the greatest areas of impact upon church life is the practice of biblical exposition.[124] As these young leaders toss out the proverbial "bathwater" of modernism, they are in danger of also tossing out the "baby" of authentic Spiritual formation through biblical preaching.

Brian McLaren is "hailed as the leader of the emergent church."[125] *Time* Magazine listed Brian McLaren as one of the twenty-five most influential evangelical leaders in the United States today.[126] Speaking of preaching in the postmodern context, he writes (quoting Walter Brueggemann),

> What is needed, [Bruggemann] says, is a new kind of preaching, preaching that opens "out the good news of the gospel with alternative modes of speech," that is "dramatic, artistic, capable of inviting persons to join in another conversation, free of the reason of technique, unencumbered by ontologies that grow abstract, unembarrassed about concreteness."[127]

Daryl Johnson responds,

> That's biblical preaching. That's what we're trying to do; taking a text, living in that text, inviting

123   Robert Webber, The Younger Evangelicals: Facing the Challenges of the New World (Grand Rapids, MI: Baker Books, 2002).
124   The terms "exposition" and "expository preaching" are used here to indicate the act of exposing an audience to the exegeted text of the Christian Scriptures. See Chapter 2.
125   Stan Grenz in a panel discussion on the teachings of Brian McLaren at Regent College, Vancouver, BC, Feb. 2005.
126   The Twenty-Five Most Influential Evangelicals in America (Time Magazine, February 7, 2005).
127   Brian McLaren, A Generous Orthodoxy (Grand Rapids, MI: Youth Specialties Books, Zondervan, 2004), 146.

other people into that text, and allowing the text to speak its Word to us as unencumbered as possible by our distortions. It would take as many forms as there are personalities, and rhetorical skill sets. On the one hand [McLaren] is saying something new because of homiletics in the last century, but nothing new in terms of what the Church has been trying to do.[128]

Brian McLaren has been a target of criticism[129] and has been unfairly labeled a "liberal."[130] McLaren is personally committed to his understanding of orthodox Christianity, expressed in a new way because it is now found in a new cultural setting. His first book challenges the reader to "reinvent the Church."[131] This, he argues, comes from the necessity of the emergence of this culture into the postmodern mindset. This can make conservative critics very nervous. They may ask, How must the Church "reinvent" itself? The real task for each generation is to guard the true Church from its compromise with culture. The Church is not anti-culture. Yet the Church stands as a prophetic voice of truth into every culture. The Church is God's covenant community in every time and culture, confirming and engaging God's presence and truth while correcting and rebuking the lies inherent in every time and culture. Rather than "reinventing" itself, the Church is to be what the Church authentically is in our generation. The Church needs to throw over the cultural baggage of the last generation, but there is always the danger of picking up what could be worse baggage from our own generation.

---

128   Panel discussion on the teachings of Brian McLaren at Regent College, Vancouver, BC, Feb. 2005.

129   See especially D.A. Carson's Becoming Conversant with the Emergent Church (Grand Rapids, MI: Zondervan, 2005)

130   See John MacArthur's comments on http://www.apprising.org/archives/2006/02/brian_mclaren_t.html

131   Brian McLaren, The Church on the Other Side: Doing Ministry in the Postmodern Matrix (Grand Rapids, MI: Zondervan, 2000), 7.

Brian McLaren's second book is written in the form of a novel.[132] His fictional characters interact with the hard issues of emergent faith. This gives him the ability to explore these ideas without the burden of having to own them. A church pastor (Dan) meets a Christian high school science teacher (Neo) who has embraced the postmodern worldview. Neo is trying to reconcile this emergent paradigm with his own evangelical beliefs. Pastor Dan represents the Christian mind "emerging" from the prison of modernism. Neo takes Dan on a journey of both friendship and philosophy as he challenges Dan to examine his own belief structure to determine which of his beliefs are truly Christian and which may be purely and only modernist heresies.

In a panel discussion of McLaren's book *Generous Orthodoxy*, Stan Grenz (whom Robert Webber called "the theologian of the new Evangelicals")[133] said,

> Like my colleagues, I am a little concerned about Brian [McLaren]'s use of the concept of "emergent." And I'm concerned about it for two reasons. First, I'm not really sure that what we get in the outworking of the book [*A Generous Orthodoxy*] is in fact what emergent theory is really saying.… There seems to be, at times, a Hegelian dimension, rather than an emergent dimension. So, I question whether he's true to emergent theory. And secondly, with respect to that, I'm not convinced that "emergent" is in fact the best metaphor to use to speak about the Church's embeddedness in its culture and the trajectory of the Church. I think more in terms of how each generation must seek to embody the one Church of Jesus Christ in the context of which it

132   Brian McLaren, A New Kind of Christian: A Tale of Two Friends on a Spiritual Journey (San Francisco, CA: Jossy-Bass, 2001).
133   Robert Webber, The Younger Evangelicals: Facing the Challenges of the New World (Grand Rapids, MI: Baker Books, 2002).

finds itself. Which is quite different I think, than the "emergent" metaphor.[134]

The "emergent" metaphor is one of evolution. Are emergent churches a legitimate evolution of the authentic Church of Jesus Christ, or are they illegitimate compromises with their embedded cultural context? Vincent Donovan, Roman Catholic missionary to Africa, argued for a kind of evolution when he wrote,

> In working with … people … do not try to call them back to where they were, and do not try to call them to where you are, as beautiful as that place might seem to you. You must have the courage to go with them to a place that neither you nor they have ever been before[135]

Are emergent church leaders going with their people to an authentically Christian place the Church has never been before? What are the implications of this to the regular practice of biblical exposition in Spiritual formation? Stan Grenz describes an e-mail he received from an acquaintance who is establishing an emergent church in Reno, Nevada. The church leaders have "five values" they will use to guide their new emergent community. These values are as follows:

1. *Mystery*—We're learning that there can be fewer answers and more questions when it comes to God, life, and life with God. And, we're OK with that.

2. *Beauty*—We celebrate artistic responses to a passionate, creative God.

3. *Conversations*—We value every person's story because every person's story is valued by God.

---

134   Panel discussion on the teachings of Brian McLaren at Regent College, Vancouver, BC, Feb. 2005.
135   Vincent J. Donovan, Christianity Rediscovered (Maryknoll, NY: Orbis Books, 2003).

4. 4. *Organic*—We are real people living in a real world trying to make a real difference with no strings attached.

5. 5. *Chicala* [*sic*]—a cool Indian word for past, present, and future; a merger of ancient or historical Christian faith and our emerging culture.[136]

This list does not include any clear affirmation of solidarity with the timeless authentic practice of raising Christians to maturity through the regular exposition of the Holy Scriptures. There is a great divide in the Western evangelical Church. Two extremes seem to vie for legitimacy in the practice of preaching in the contemporary evangelical Church in the West. On the one extreme are those who would champion what has been known as "biblical [or expository] preaching" as the authentic approach to Christian proclamation, whether people will (or can) listen or not. On the other extreme are those who have rejected what they see as a modernist paradigm and are attempting to craft a truly postmodern approach to Christian Spiritual formation. This emergent movement emphasizes the need to change the style of public weekly church proclamation to make it more listener-centered and palatable, sometimes whether the message of God's Word is heard or not.

Tom Sine asks, "Is it possible the church is in crisis and no one noticed? Is it possible God is raising up a new generation to re-invent the church?"[137] There is a movement of young postmodern emergent churches growing in the West, led by twenty- to thirty-year-old Christians.[138] These churches are forging new communities with unique expressions of Christian faith. The young leaders of

---

136   Stan Grenz, panel discussion on the teachings of Brian McLaren at Regent College, Vancouver, BC, Feb. 2005.

137   Quoted from a pamphlet for a "Mustard Seed Associates" conference called "Does the Future Have a Church?" (Jan. 17–19, 2003). This conference is for "those disconnected with the status quo. It is for younger and older Christians who want to create ways to engage the new challenges of a world caught in cultural shift." (http://www.msainfo.org/date.asp?schedule=58&MainID=265).

138   Tom and Christine Sine have traveled throughout the West, connecting with young churches. They have created a virtual community through the Internet to encourage and learn from these "emerging church" leaders (www.msainfo.org).

these emergent churches are rejecting the modernist, rationalistic paradigm inherent in contemporary Western churches. Meanwhile, they are attempting to craft truly postmodern approaches to Christian Spiritual formation. This is especially true of their attitude towards and practice of preaching. They are emphasizing the need to change the style of public weekly church proclamation, and to make it more palatable to a postmodern audience. But what will this new approach look like, and will it be an authentically Christian expression?

The emergent church is a potent force in Western Christianity.[139] What kinds of experiments are being done in these emerging churches, and which of these experiments will best reflect an authentic expression of the Christian Church in contemporary society? Eugene Cho, lead pastor of "Quest," a postmodern church in Seattle, writes,

> There are several things that we do know about the future of the church: 1) the future is uncertain, 2) there will be many changes, and 3) it will not be an easy journey. But as the world changes ... we must be proactive in our desire to engage the culture with the love and truth of Jesus Christ. Some things that need to be understood clearly is the fact that we no longer live in what sociologists call a "Christian dominant" culture. Whereas the Church existed and thrived throughout the majority of the United States history, they are now in a very crucial stage as we enter this new century. Statistically, about 70,000 of the 350,000 churches that existed in the US have closed their doors in the past 20 years. 30% of churchgoers today are over 60 years old and perhaps, more alarmingly, the generation that comprises the 18–35 age group has fallen sharply in their church attendance—from 36-27% in the

---

139   Only 5 percent of churches in Canada draw over five hundred people. This makes The Place, at over six hundred, a "megachurch" and it is therefore having an impact on the broader church scene in the nation.

past 10 years. Furthermore, 80–85% of mainline churches are in "serious" decline. Even despite the fact that there are waves of churches being planted throughout the United States, for every church that is being planted, three churches are being shut down. The hard and cold fact is that the church has lost its relevance and ability to communicate to a fast changing and postmodern generation.[140]

Cho recognizes that there is a paradox today; there is a profound "spiritual" hunger in the emerging generation, while the Christian Church continues to shrink in the West. In her research and interviews with over five hundred Christian young people in the United States, Colleen Carroll found a widespread embrace of the "orthodox" Christian faith among this generation.[141] Carroll states, "I was surprised by just how widespread this trend [towards embracing orthodox Christianity] was, how deep it runs in the culture."[142] This is especially surprising in an age in which any authoritarian dogma is denigrated. Yet one must ask, What is this "orthodoxy" that is being embraced? Orthodoxy has traditionally been forged in the Christian Church through the exegetical study and public exposition of the Bible. How are emerging church leaders using preaching in their provision of theological foundations for Christian formation for this next generation?

Doug Pagitt, pastor of "Solomon's Porch" in Minneapolis, told the 1,100 participants at a conference on emergent churches in San Diego that "preaching is broken."[143] He warned that people today are distrustful of authority figures "with overarching explanations of how the world works." He called a sermon "a violent act" because "it's a violence toward the will of the people who have to sit there and take it." He said that such preaching "creates an artificial distance with the congregation." It is fair to criticize the ways that preaching practices

---

140   Eugene Cho, lead pastor at Quest Church (http://www.seaq.org).

141   Colleen Carroll, The New Faithful: Why Young Adults are Embracing Christian Orthodoxy (Plano, TX: Loyola Press, 2002).

142   Interview with Colleen Carroll in Christianity Today (August 5, 2002).

143   Tom Allan, "Is our Preaching Out of Touch?" Faithworks Magazine (July 2004).

are held prisoner to a modernist or a premodernist paradigm. But does Pagitt offer an alternative way to authentically do the vital work of exposing God's people to his Word in a postmodern way?

The shift from a modernist worldview in Western culture to a postmodern one has been so seismic that Western churches are left grappling with unstable ground. The choice seems to be between the shifting uncertainties of a vision for what an authentic postmodern Christian Church will look like and (as some would argue) the irrelevance of continuing to function as a modernist Church. These two scenarios represent a crisis in the practice of preaching in Western churches today.

As contemporary pastors, congregations, and denominations grapple with the radical cultural impact of postmodernism on Western churches, there are basically two dominant responses in the practice of preaching. On the one hand there are those who are entrenched in a modernist approach to classical expository preaching, while on the other hand there are those who are experimenting with new, purely postmodern forms of public proclamation.

Entrenched churches assume a level of commitment and understanding from their members, while the experimental churches assume that their members are transient and unaffiliated. The former group tends to be from an older generation that is more loyal in its church attendance. The latter group tends to be from a younger generation with a shrinking or non-existent church attendance tradition.[144] Some churches in the former group are trying to engage the postmodern world by augmenting their regular church services with some emergent methodology. True emergent churches, meanwhile, see themselves as completely breaking with modernist church methodologies altogether.[145] Os Guinness warns,

---

144   The 2001 Canadian Religious Census indicates that the population of those attending traditional churches in Canada is a rapidly aging one. With a median age of 37.3 in Canada, the median age of Protestants is 41.9, while the median age of those with "no religion" is 31.1. 74.3 percent of those who claim "no religion" are under forty-five, while only 25.7 percent of Canadians over forty-five claim to have "no religion."

145   Richard W. Flory and Donald E. Miller, Gen X Religion (Routledge, NY: 2000), 231–249.

"This desire to be fashionable is exactly why Christians are now becoming marginalized."[146]

There have been many publications on the subject of preaching, and many on the subject of the paradigm shift from modernism to postmodernism in the Western world. Yet there is very little that has been written on the subject of what authentic Christian preaching looks like in this postmodern context. Very little has been written taking the authenticity of Spiritual formation through preaching to the historic faith community seriously, and also taking the unique demands of this contemporary Western context seriously. In this chapter, I first examine the literature that explores the issues of the postmodern context and its impact on the Church.

There are few critical publications that discuss contemporary theory and practices of expository preaching as central to our congregants' lifelong Christian formation. Instead, there is a plethora of books, articles, journals, and conferences encouraging churches to be more "seeker sensitive" or "missional." In *The Missional Church*, Darrill L. Guder argues that the Church in the West has moved from being the formative institution at the center of society to being a missional movement that engages culture on the periphery of society.[147]

John Van Stolten of New Hope Christian Reformed Church in Calgary, Alberta, has a church of three hundred postmoderns. He gives topical talks on contemporary issues, illustrated with scenes from popular films or episodes of *The Simpsons*. He says they'll "never do a series on the Book of Revelation."[148] Why not? Are churches trying to reach out to a new generation through "dumbing down"[149] the message and practice of being Church? If emerging churches in the West are merely missional outreach vehicles, then where and how will the lifelong theological formation of God's

---

146   Quoted in an interview with Dick Staub in Christianity and Renewal Magazine, http://www.christianitytoday.com/ct/2003/134/22.0.html (accessed August 25, 2003).
147   Darrill L. Guder and Lois Barrett, The Missional Church: A Vision for the Sending of the Church in North America (Grand Rapids, MI: William B. Eerdmans Publishing Company, 1998).
148   Calgary Herald, January 27, 2001.
149   Marva Dawn warns against this trend in her book Reaching Out Without Dumbing Down: A Theology of Worship for the Turn-of-the-Century Culture (William B. Eerdmans Publishing Company, 1995).

people happen? This has traditionally happened through the regular exposition of the Scriptures through preaching.[150] Peter Adam writes, "Christian gospel ministry involves explaining, preaching, applying and interpreting this sufficient Word so that people may be converted and congregations may be built up in faith, godliness and usefulness."[151]

How are believers being theologically formed in emerging churches? In the face of shrinking traditional church numbers and growing disdain for preaching in contemporary Western society, what is the philosophy and practice of preaching among emerging church leaders? Are the leaders of emergent churches rejecting what may be a style of institutional speaking, which is merely a product of the modernist age? One must ask, what is it being replaced with? If the modernist approach to preaching is being scorned, what is an authentically Christian approach to public proclamation in the postmodern church context? What part of the modernist approach to preaching is the proverbial "bathwater" that must be tossed out, while the Church keeps the "baby" of authentic biblical exposition?

Does Preaching have a Place Anymore?

Does preaching have a vital place in the future of the Western, postmodern Church? Is expository preaching the authentic approach to public proclamation? Hadden Robinson says, "When you talk about expository preaching, you're not primarily talking about the form of the sermon. You are really talking about a philosophy."[152]

---

150   This is reflected, for instance, in the Anglican Form of Ordaining or Consecrating of an Archbishop or Bishop (1662). Question: Are you persuaded that the Holy Scriptures contain sufficiently all doctrine required of necessity for eternal salvation through faith in Jesus Christ? And are you determined out of the same Holy Scriptures to instruct people committed to your charge, and to teach or maintain nothing as required of necessity to eternal salvation, but that which you shall be persuaded may be concluded and proved by the same? Answer: I am so persuaded and have so determined by God's grace.

151   Peter Adams, "The Preacher and the Sufficient Word," When God's Voice is Heard (Downers Grove, IL: Intervarsity Press, 1995),

152   Robinson, Preaching Magazine.

What is the authentically biblical philosophy that undergirds the public practice of preaching in the life of the Church? Is expository preaching a prisoner of modernity, being "rationalistic, elitist, authoritarian and unbiblical"?[153] What should authentic Christian preaching look like in the postmodern context?

There is a need to understand what is happening in the broad emerging church scene in the West, especially in the area of the weekly practice of public proclamation. There is much that can be learned from a postmodern awareness and reaction to modernism that may lead Western churches towards a more authentic practice of faith expression. What will be the place of biblical proclamation in that authentic practice? Is there a postmodern style of preaching that is authentically Christian, which authentically preaches the formative *logos* of God in the contemporary *ethos* of Western culture? If so, what will authentic Christian preaching look like in the postmodern context? Is there a biblical model of the ministry of preaching? How are emerging church leaders responding to the challenge of engaging a contemporary culture that disdains preaching?

In the book *Mastering Contemporary Preaching*,[154] Bill Hybels, Stuart Briscoe, and Haddon Robinson have attempted to investigate the issue of preaching in this postmodern context. But they fail to penetrate beyond a discussion of mere preaching styles and miss the opportunity to discuss what the essential nature and purpose of preaching ought to be in this and every age, the proclamation of God's formative Word. This can also be said of David Henderson's book *Culture Shift*.[155] Though the book provides excellent ways to address important contemporary topics, it does not answer the underlying questions of why preach at all, or what role preaching plays in Spiritual formation.

Likewise, Richard Eslinger's book, *A New Hearing*,[156] alleges to be a serious investigation into five "effective" contemporary

---

153   Hilborn, 174.
154   Bill Hybels, Stuart Briscoe, and Haddon Robinson, Mastering Contemporary Preaching (Portland, OR: Multnomah Press, 1989).
155   David Henderson, Culture Shift: Communicating God's Truth in a Changing World (Grand Rapids, MI: Baker Book House Company, 1999).
156   Richard Eslinger, A New Hearing (Nashville, TN: Abingdon Press, 1987).

preachers. However, Eslinger does not give any kind of theological or theoretical criteria for comparing these five preachers, or for answering the question of why these five preachers should be considered "effective" at all. The reader is left wondering what the essence of preaching (the proverbial "baby") fundamentally is, how one can objectively evaluate what is "good" preaching as opposed to what is "bad," or what authentic preaching ought to look like in this new postmodern Western context, as opposed to what it should not be (the proverbial "bathwater").

Writers have articulated the reality of the monumental shift in our Western Church context from a modernist worldview to a new postmodern one. The Western Church has been so associated with the modernist paradigm of culture and belief that it is no longer seen as relevant. History shows that this is a struggle the Church has faced during each epochal change in its social context.[157] Walter Truett Anderson writes, "We are in the midst of a great, confusing, stressful, and enormously promising historical transition, and it has to do with a change not so much in what we believe as in how we believe."[158]

This situation continues to lead the Church further away from her missional purpose. Alan Roxburgh writes,

> "Unless … leaders recognize and understand the extent to which they and their congregations have been marginalized in modernity, they will not meaningfully shape the direction of congregational life for missionary engagement."[159]

Douglas J. Hall is pessimistic about any attempt to retain any cultural control or relevance if the Church remains tied to

157   Robert Webber, Ancient-Future Evangelism: Making Your Church a Faith-Forming Community (Grand Rapids, MI: Baker Books, 2003).
158   Walt Anderson, The Truth About the Truth: De-Confusing and Re-Constructing Truth, A New Consciousness Reader (NY: G.P. Putnam's Sons, 1995).
159   Alan Roxburgh, The Missionary Congregation, Leadership, and Liminality Christian Mission and Modern Culture (Valley Forge, PA: Trinity Press International, 1997).

the modernist worldview. Meanwhile, he remains hopeful for new opportunities for the authentic Christian faith to engage the contemporary, post-Constantinian Western culture.[160] To do this he underlines "four worldly quests" through which "Christians may engage their society from the perspective of faith and hope." These "quests" are the search for "moral authenticity," "meaningful community," "transcendence and mystery," and "meaning."[161] Yet his primary argument is for Christian pastors to regain their prophetic ministry of being pastoral poets who concentrate on proclaiming God's Word, saying, "Ministers are recalled to the teaching office."[162]

Writing from many years of teaching about the mission of the church, and from his own observation of the direction of the church today, Eddie Gibbs offers many excellent insights. He gives concrete suggestions for how the Western Church cannot only grow, but can turn the tide of history from becoming a marginalized ancient institution of religion to becoming an instrument of vibrant change in our culture.[163] He describes how the Church can move from living in the past to engaging the present, from being market driven to being mission oriented, from following celebrities to encountering saints, from holding dead orthodoxy to nurturing living faith, and from attracting a crowd to seeking the lost. However, his lack of vision for a Church led by the proclamation of the living Word of God is disappointing.

Gibbs' suggestion that the Church needs to move from "dead orthodoxy" to "living faith" is suspect. Can orthodoxy be dead? This is the crucial question as one is constantly tempted to alter the truth, or right-thinking (*ortho-doxios*), to suit a postmodern palate. It is unpopular to adhere to the regular obedience and instruction of God's Word. One would rather listen to the latest instruction on marriage enrichment or stock tips or self-improvement plans. Gibbs'

---

160   Douglas J. Hall, The End of Christendom and the Future of Christianity (Harrisburg, PA: Trinity Press, 1995).

161   Hall, 57.

162   Hall, 49.

163   Eddie Gibbs, Church Next: Quantum Changes in Christian Ministry [New ed.] (Leicester, UK: Inter-Varsity Press, 2000).

definition of "church" seems to focus too much on the Sunday morning service, and his definition of "worship" on the singing during that service. He does offer some helpful suggestions for proactive strategies for Western churches. But he lacks an emphasis on the ministry of preaching as the prophetic leading of the people of God and the communication tool for outreach to the lost.

Michael Frost and Alan Hirsch offer what is fast becoming a benchmark for how the Church can authentically represent the Christian message to a postmodern context.[164] They argue for a contextualization of the Christian message, and for the Church to be a missional body. Yet they offer no clear explanation or demonstration for how that message is authentically proclaimed in the regular practice of the Church.

Christian futurist Leonard Sweet calls for many new and innovative ways of expressing the Christian faith in this postmodern context. He argues for the Western Church to rediscover its meaning, mission, and purpose by forming new methods for doing church by using some old methods. This "ancient future faith" is "a faith that is both ancient and future, both historical and contemporary … and attempt[s] to show the church how to camp in the future in the light of the past."[165]

In his many popular books, Sweet expresses a commitment to the Bible as authoritative and important to authentic Christian spirituality.[166] Yet he offers very little to describe how authentic biblical exposition can actually be practiced in postmodern churches. His many books merely offer critiques of modernist approaches to Bible teaching. Likewise, Pete Ward argues, "The theology and values of the Church are not up for grabs."[167] Yet he gives us little clarity for

---

164   Michael Frost and Alan Hirsch, The Shaping of Things to Come: Innovation and Mission for the 21st Century Church (Peabody, MA: Hendrickson Publishers, 2003).

165   Leonard Sweet, Post-Modern Pilgrims: First Century Passion for the 21st Century World (Nashville, TN: Broadman & Holman, 2000).

166   See especially Aqua Church (Grand Rapids, MI: Zondervan, 1999), Soul Salsa (Grand Rapids, MI: Zondervan, 2000), Postmodern Pilgrims (Nashville, TN: Broadman & Holman, 2000), and Carpe Manana (Grand Rapids, MI: Zondervan, 2001).

167   Peter Ward, Mass Culture: Eucharist and Mission in a Post-Modern World (Oxford, UK: Bible Reading Fellowship, 1999), 15.

a theology or value of biblical exposition that transcends the age. George Cladis offers a list of nine characteristics of postmodernity. Yet he gives us no explanation for how this new social paradigm calls for a new kind of proclamation in our churches.

David Hilborn declared that a modernist style of "expository preaching" is a prisoner of modernity, being "rationalistic, elitist, authoritarian, and unbiblical,"[168] but an emergent compromise with postmodern culture can be a prisoner to our youth-oriented postmodern culture. Duffy Robbins writes,

> I'm concerned that our youth ministry culture has the same kind of adolescent arrogance that thirty years ago led to the maxim, "Never trust anyone over thirty," except that now it's "Never trust anyone who doesn't define himself as *postmodern.*" Unfortunately, that kind of narrow chronological and ideological landscape leaves us vulnerable to momentary fads and fashions."[169]

Darrill L. Guder advocates that the Western Church see itself as a peripheral movement, engaging its culture as a missional movement. If "missional" means "missionary outreach to those outside", where and how is the maturing of those already inside happening? If the church service becomes primarily an outreach event, is it still Church? What about the identity of the Church as the peculiar called out ones whose primary task is to worship God? Some descriptions of what some emergent churches are doing seem more like a youth evangelism enterprise than a church. Marva J. Dawn describes this as "dumbing down" the Church.[170] If emerging churches are primarily missional outreach vehicles, how and where will believing Christians be raised to maturity in Christian community? The regular exposition of

---

168   David Hilborn, Picking up the Pieces (London, UK: Hodder & Stoughton, 1997).
169   http://www.youthspecialties.com/articles/topics/postmodernism/adolescence.php
170   Marva J. Dawn, Reaching Out Without Dumbing Down (Grand Rapids, MI: William B. Eerdmans Publishing Company, 1995).

the Scriptures through preaching has been a vital element in the formation of the Church and Christian people.[171]

John Wallis is on the editorial team for www.next-wave.org, an Internet magazine that is engaging the emerging community. In an e-mail he writes about his emergent acquaintances,

> I wonder if any of them even preach anymore. Most of the people I know are involved or leading missional communities, and I am not sure preaching as you are describing in your survey happens anymore. The first question made me stop. Most of the people I know are in communites [*sic*] that are less than 30. I still attend a large suburban church and [*sic*] not sure why at times, [*sic*] hear preaching every week from a gifted speaker but there is usually something missing. I sometimes wonder if preaching will slowly die out. I think it is starting to in missional communities maybe not, or maybe it has just taken another form. [172]

It is because of the shortcomings of a primarily "missional" church that Stan Grenz argues that there is

> An insufficient understanding of the role of doctrine in Christian life, or in formation of Christian identity ... being Apostolic in doctrine is crucial to Christian identity, both as a community, as well as each of us as individual Christians.[173]

---

171   D. M. Lloyd-Jones wrote, "Is it not clear as you take a bird's-eye view of Church history, that the decadent periods and eras in the history of the Church have always been those periods when preaching had declined? What is it that always heralds the dawn of a Reformation or of a Revival? It is renewed preaching." Preaching and Preachers (London, UK: Hodder & Stoughton, 1971), 24.

172   From an e-mail to me dated July 19, 2003.

173   Stan Granz, panel discussion on the teachings of Brian McLaren at Regent College, Vancouver, BC, Feb. 2005.

In his book *The Preacher's Portrait*,[174] John Stott uses five biblical words to expertly examine the cross-generational attributes and responsibilities of a Christian preacher. He is a *steward*, a *herald*, a *witness*, a *father*, and a *servant*. The *steward* is the metaphor that best helps in examining the function of preaching in every age. A *steward* cares for another's goods in trust. He does not own the goods himself. He dispenses the other's goods as the other demands. He also serves the other's guests. The owner's guests have not come to visit with the *steward*; they have come to visit the owner and to be served by the *steward* along with the owner. The Word of God is entrusted to Christians. It does not belong to anyone. It belongs to God. Preachers in every generation must care for it in trust and dispense it with reverence and awe to those who gather to listen to his Word. Christians desire to hear the Word of their Master. Christians would be most disobedient *stewards* to serve the Master's guests our own measly goods or our Master's goods pretending they are our own. In *I Believe in Preaching*, Stott writes,

> Preaching is indispensable to Christianity. Without preaching a necessary part of its authenticity has been lost. For Christianity is, in its very essence, a religion of the Word of God. No attempt to understand Christianity can succeed which overlooks or denies the truth that the living God has taken the initiative to reveal himself savingly to fallen humanity; or that his self-revelation has been given by the most straightforward means of communication known to us, namely by word and words; or that he calls upon those who have heard his Word to speak it to others.[175]

One popular compromise with postmodern culture is the rejection of expository preaching because it is seen as too methodological. It

---

174   John Stott, The Preacher's Portrait: Some New Testament Word Studies (Grand Rapids, MI: William B. Eerdmans Publishing Company, 1961).
175   John Stott, I Believe in Preaching (London, UK: Hodder and Stoughton, 1982), 15.

is true that when any spiritual exercise in the Church—including the exposition of Scripture—is reduced to techniques, it destroys the authenticity of the Church. James Houston writes,

> What is destroying Christianity is the marketeering of Christianity.... Disciple-making is not about replicable, transferable methods, but about the mystery of two walking together. Methods treat discipleship as a problem to be solved, but mentoring treats discipleship as a relationship to be lived.[176]

Whether it is mentoring or preaching, the authentic work of Church leaders is to do what they have always been called to do. But they must do it by the Spirit in the context of their present culture. Leonard Sweet argues, "Christians should not embrace a postmodern worldview; we must not adapt to postmodernity ... but we do need to incarnate the timeless in the timely."[177] What would this look like in a postmodern context?

---

176   James Houston, "Making Disciples, Not Just Converts: Evangelism without Discipleship Dispenses Cheap Grace," editorial in Christianity Today Magazine, October 25, 1999, 28.
177   Leonard I. Sweet, Post-Modern Pilgrims: First Century Passion for the 21st Century World (Nashville, TN: Broadman & Holman, 2000).

Chapter 4
The Conveyor of Spiritual Formation

The Perception of the Contemporary Audience

Using a theological framework for understanding the essence of authentic Christian Spiritual formation through biblical preaching, I have demonstrated that the fundamental task of the spiritual leader has always and only been to listen to God's Word, to understand God's meaning through careful exegesis, and to proclaim it faithfully to his contemporary community. The Christian leader must proclaim the texts of God's Word, the Bible. This is how believers have been theologically and morally formed in every generation.

Using a sociological framework for understanding the shift from a modernist to a postmodernist worldview, I have demonstrated that a movement of young, postmodern churches is emerging in the West. The leaders of these emergent churches are developing new approaches to expressing the authentic Christian faith. In the West, these leaders are operating in a predominantly post-Christian environment with its own unique new language, culture, and history. This will have a profound effect on the Christian leader's approach to Spiritual formation.

Using a theoretical framework for understanding contextualization in public communication, I have argued that the three rhetorical elements of *logos, ethos,* and *pathos* must be attended to in the use of preaching in Spiritual formation for authentic communication to occur. The *logos* of Christian preaching will always be the authentically understood message of the texts of God's Word. Its message will not change. It cannot mean what it never meant.

The *ethos* of the receiving audience will change dramatically from one generation and one region to another. The content of the eternal *logos* of the Word of God has always needed to be contextualized into the contextual *ethos* of new languages, cultures, and histories by authentic conveyors who speak with the *pathos* of perceived integrity.

The *pathos* of the conveyor of Christian Spiritual formation will always need to be perceived by his contemporary audience as having integrity worth listening to. Though each generation will have subtle differences in interpreting true integrity, the conveyor must have it in the eyes of his listeners, or he will not be heard at all.

A Research Study

In 1999, I conducted a research study to explore the attitudes and practice of emergent leaders in the area of preaching. The data demonstrates how these emerging church leaders understand the postmodern context and its influence on their ministry and preaching. It reveals how these emerging church leaders attempt to contextualize their sermons and how this contextualization is especially reflected within the praxis of their preaching. It also shows how biblical truth is incorporated into the meetings of their postmodern congregations, and how the actual practices of preaching reflect the practical, theological, and philosophical perspectives of these representative leaders. The scope of this study was to determine an answer to the question, What is the attitude towards and practice of expository preaching among emergent church leaders?

The Conceptual Framework

This study was a qualitative investigation using surveys and interviews to investigate how certain young Western emergent church leaders understand the role and practice of preaching within the context of their postmodern congregations. Dr. Lori Carrell wrote *The Great American Sermon Survey* (Wheaton, IL: Mainstay Church Resources, 2000). This may be called the Minor Postmodern Sermon Survey.

As a qualitative research project, the sample was intentionally small (ten respondents) and nonrandom. I was the primary instrument of the research through the surveys, interviews, observations, and analysis. These tools were intentionally interactive and inductive. The goal of the research was to understand and describe the phenomenological inquiry, and to offer a comprehensive and expansive hypothesis for future research and practice.

The Exploratory Approach

The goal of this study was to investigate the essential attitudes and approaches to preaching among leaders of Western emergent churches. The secondary research questions were as follows:

1. How do some emerging church leaders understand the postmodern context and its influence on ministry and preaching?

2. How do emerging church leaders attempt to contextualize their sermons?

3. How is this contextualization reflected within their praxis of preaching?

4. How is biblical truth incorporated into the meeting of a postmodern congregation?

5. How do the actual practices of preaching reflect practical, theological, and philosophical perspectives?

As discussed in Chapter 3, there is an apparent lack of exploration of emergent practices in preaching in light of both authentically postmodern and authentically biblical preaching concerns. There are studies in preaching methods.[178] There are studies on the effects of postmodernity on the Western Church.[179] There are also studies on the emergent church phenomenon.[180] But there is little that explores what is actually thought and practiced among emergent church leaders in the area of regular biblical exposition. This lack of previous substantive study warranted the use of an exploratory approach to seek out new insights and assess these issues from a fresh perspective.

The exploratory approach was most helpful for investigating the issues surrounding the meaning of the practice of preaching in the emergent church.[181] Through direct contact with leaders of Western emergent churches, these leaders described their practice and experience firsthand, providing valuable research data for categorization and exploration. This data was used to explore the research questions for this study and to identify important issues for future study.

The emphasis of this investigation was to record and analyze the insights and experiences of emergent church leaders who are directly involved in attempts to successfully engage postmodern church attendees with biblical messages. The exploratory method of the initial surveys provided material for follow-up interviews. The individual interviews provided an open dialogue with these church leaders, allowing them to articulate their insights and observations in response to a casual conversation with me, in order to explore how

---

178   See David Buttrick, Homiletic: Moves and Structures (Philadelphia, PA: Fortress Press, 1988).

179   See Stanley Grenz, A Primer on Postmodernism. (Grand Rapids, MI: William B. Eerdmans Publishing Company, 1996).

180   See Dan Kimball, The Emerging Church: Vintage Christianity for New Generations (Grand Rapids, MI: Zondervan, 2003).

181   R. R. Sherman and R. B. Webb, "Qualitative Research in Education: A Focus." in R. R. Sherman and R. B. Webb (eds.), Qualitative Research in Education: Focus and Methods (Bristol, PA: Falmer Press, 1988), 7.

these emerging church leaders understand the postmodern context and its influence on their preaching.

The Qualitative Method

The goal of exploring the respondents' context, setting, and frame of reference was best suited to the qualitative methodology.[182] I developed a survey (Appendix A) and used it to gather initial data. The survey consisted of three parts: the respondent's church data, the respondent's personal data, and the respondent's preaching habits data. This information gave me descriptive data that stressed the context, education, and experience of each respondent. The survey was targeted to gather data specifically from emergent leaders of Western, postmodern congregations.

The survey data provided me with essential information on each participant and a variety of data for comparison between them. I used the survey to look for a representation not only of emergent churches, but also various church sizes, different countries, and both sexes. Meanwhile, the survey data gave me initial insights into the respondents' attitudes toward and practices in the area of preaching. Survey question A:4 provided a glimpse into the average time preaching takes in the respondents' regular church meeting. This gave me some indication of the importance of preaching to each respondent. Question B:3 provided a record of the respondents' level of theological education. This familiarized me with the intensity of the respondents' academic experience and expertise. Questions C:1–C:7 informed me on each respondent's regular preaching habits. Of greatest importance were the insights into the awareness and handling of the biblical texts practiced by each respondent.

The surveys were followed up by interviews with a representative group of ten respondents to gather more in-depth, qualitative data through a "conversation with a purpose"[183] with each respondent.

182   C. Marshall and G. B. Rossman, Designing Qualitative Research (Thousand Oaks, CA: SAGE Publishing, 1989), 4.

183   L. A. Dexter, Elite and Specialized Interviewing (Evanston, IL: Northwestern

I developed a list of specific questions (Appendix B) to further investigate the subjective viewpoints of the respondents, especially on issues relating to preaching to postmoderns. The interviews involved a mix of "highly structured and informal" questions.[184]

These interview questions were each designed to acquire greater insight into the attitudes and practices around the area of preaching through the interviewees' own words. Question one was designed to allow the respondents to describe the formative influences that had shaped the foundations of their attitudes and practices. Questions two and three were designed to elicit spontaneous responses to the phrase "biblical preaching." I quoted back to the respondent his or her own written responses from the survey, with these follow-up questions, to gather more verbal data. These questions provided rich responses around the respondents' attitudes towards preaching and their personal struggles to do it in their settings.

Questions four, five, and six were designed to provide data on the specific personal habits these respondents practiced in their sermon preparation. Along with the previously acquired survey data on time spent in sermon preparation, and the long-range development of their future sermon plans, these interview questions allowed the respondents to paint the picture of their own regular routines and resources around the sermonic process.

The answers to questions seven, eight, and nine provided data on the respondents' attitudes toward "expository preaching." Here, I was looking for the respondents to give their reactions to this discipline, as well as their definition of "expository preaching" and their insights into its ongoing practice or abandonment in the emergent church setting.

Question ten provided data on the respondents' idea of the most important task of a leader in the "emerging church." These responses offer rich material on the priorities of these ten individuals, as well as a glimpse into the priorities of the emergent church. Each interview was recorded and transcribed for further analysis. I used

---

University Press, 1970), 136.

184   S. B. Merriam, *Qualitative Research and Case Study Applications in Education* (San Francisco, CA: Jossy-Bass Publishers, 1998), 73.

this material to determine the nature of the attitudes and practices of the preaching ministries among these representative emergent church leaders.

The Sampling

The qualitative sampling process "involves the selection of research site, time, people and events."[185] Using a broad sampling grid, I attempted to gather data from an open representation of Western countries. This choice of probabilistic sampling[186] was made to gather non-generalized information regarding attitudes and practices of these respondents. A combination of purposive sampling[187] and convenience sampling[188] was used to gather the initial survey data. The purposive group was made up of young Western emergent church leaders who were actively engaged in the practice of preaching at the time of the study. Meanwhile, the distribution of the surveys depended on my access to a network of eligible (and willing) respondents. The convenience sample group consisted of those who volunteered to complete and return the survey.

The Data Collection

There is a loose association of emergent churches internationally. Many are connected through the Internet and conferences. I co-hosted a conference for Canadian emergent church leaders in 2003 in order to make contacts. The data collection for this study was done primarily through the Internet. Over one hundred surveys were electronically passed on to prospective respondents by e-mail.

185   R. G. Burgess (ed.), Field Research: A Source Book and Field Manual (London, UK: Allen & Unwin, 1982), 76.
186   Merriam, 61.
187   M. D. DeCompte and J. Preissle, Ethnography and Qualitative Design in Educational Research (2nd. ed.) (Orlando, FL: Academic Press, 1993), 69.
188   Merriam, 63.

I forwarded to multiple e-mail addresses the following e-mail with the survey document attached:

> I am a doctoral student at Gordon-Conwell Theological Seminary. I am doing a thesis project on "preaching" in the emergent context. Would you be willing to fill out the attached survey and return it to me by e-mail or post?

Most of these prospects were identified through emergent church websites. A few candidates were identified through individuals known to me. All prospective prospects were asked to pass the survey on to others who might be interested in participating in the study. I followed up with survey participants as they responded to me. These responses came back to me in random intervals over a period of about six months. After twenty completed surveys were collected, I sent the following e-mail to all twenty of the survey respondents:

> I don't know if you remember, but you participated in a survey on preaching for my doctoral thesis. I would like to speak with you for the next stage of my research on preaching in the emerging church. When would be a good time for you to chat on the phone for about 45 minutes in the next few weeks?

Phone interviews were then arranged over a period of another six months with those survey respondents who voluntarily continued with the study by responding and setting a time for the follow-up interview. After a representative study sample group of ten was reached, I went to the next stage of data transcription and analysis.

As a naturalistic inquiry study, my emphasis was on discovering these emergent church leaders' attitudes towards expository preaching.[189] Likewise, there was an emphasis on exploring their perspectives on the practice of preaching among other emergent

---

189   Marshall and Rossman, 127.

church leaders. The basic data I sought was the verbal responses of the participants, which provided interesting and detailed material regarding the respondents' "experiences, opinions, feelings, and knowledge"[190] of the practice of preaching being attempted in emergent churches.

The Interviewing Method

The goal of the interviews was to provide greater understanding of the material provided through the completed surveys. I directed spontaneous follow-up questions to further the enquiry into the practice of preaching among emergent churches. This method stressed the relevance of the interviewee's experience and insight into the research questions. I maintained control of the interview, however, and all the standard questions were answered, to a greater or lesser degree, by all participants. With the exception of interview question number seven, all interview questions were open ended.[191] They also provided opportunities for the interviewees to expound on their answers as they saw fit and direct the interview topics beyond the formal standard questions to provide insight into the interviewee's experiences, concerns, and opinions on the greater research question. The respondents were given freedom to act as key informants,"[192] sometimes articulating and guiding my exploration of the study.

As Dexter explains,[193] the nature of the interview is determined by certain variables. I made every attempt to remain neutral in asking these interview questions,[194] referring sometimes to the surveys directly to remind the interviewees of their survey answers. I also made an effort to avoid phrases that would expose my theological

---

190   M. Q. Patton, Qualitative Evaluation Methods (2nd. ed.) (Thousand Oaks, CA: SAGE Publishers, 1990), 10.

191   Merriam, 79.

192   Ibid, 85.

193   Dexter, 24.

194   L. Katz, "The Experience of Personal Change" (Ph.D. dissertation, Union Graduate School, Union Institute, Cincinnati, OH, 1987), 37.

or philosophical bias. I determined the details of the follow-up information requested through interview questions two and four to clarify certain material presented in the corresponding responses gathered through survey questions C:5 and C:6, respectively.

I spoke to each participant, using the standard list of questions, during a pre-arranged, forty-five minute phone call. These phone interviews were conducted over a six-month period, as participants were contacted and phone meetings could be arranged. All interviews were recorded onto a computer using an MP3 format. I also made handwritten notes during the interviews for follow-up questions and for further research to be done by me.

The Data Analysis

The data analysis of the surveys consisted of cataloguing individual statistical information for each respondent, as well as statistical averages for the study. The data analysis of the interviews consisted of examination of the elements of specific phrases and statements obtained through the survey and interview procedures. This was done from a "constant comparative" methodology.[195] The survey and interview data was organized into four thematic meaning categories[196] for synthesis, based on the theological and rhetorical foundations of this study and the emerging meanings articulated by the respondents. The four thematic categories were 1) *statistical facts*—information about each participant's personal and professional setting, including his or her church, education, and years of ministry; 2) *ethos*—the respondent's descriptions of his or her approach to understanding and engaging the language, culture, and history of context of the intended audience of the sermon; 3) *pathos*— the respondent's descriptions of his or her approach to presenting themselves as an authentic conveyor of information with perceived

---

195   B. G. Glaser and A. L. Stauss, The Discovery of Grounded Theory (Chicago, IL: Aldine Press, 1967), 37.
196   S. J. Taylor and R. Bogdan, Introduction to Qualitative Research Methods (New York, NY: Wiley Publishers, 1984), 139.

integrity; and 4) *logos*—the respondent's descriptions of his or her approach to understanding and exposing the content of the Scripture texts in a sermon preparation and presentation.

Data analysis occurred primarily after the interviews were transcribed and coded. Each survey and interview was coded into the four thematic categories for categorization and comparison. All respondents were then analyzed together under each thematic category. Each respondent was given a number to represent his or her identity in the study, in order to keep all identities anonymous.

The Methodological Credibility

This study on the practice of expository preaching among emergent church leaders sought to produce valid and reliable knowledge in an ethical manner. As a qualitative study, validity, reliability, and objectivity were maintained throughout. Internal validity[197] was maintained through capturing the actual written and verbal responses of the study participants. These responses were carefully edited to maintain the consistent contextual meaning of all responses. The interviews themselves captured the authentic shared meanings between the respondents and me. The amplified questions added to the interviews provided the opportunity for greater validity of objective understanding within the study. External validity[198] was maintained through the inclusion of reliable *statistical facts* of each respondent for the purpose of understanding similar situations, and for extending and applying this study to other events. The objectivity of this study refers primarily to the quality of the data produced through proper qualitative research procedures, rather than my personal characteristics. My personal bias was kept in check during the survey and the interview process through random sampling and keeping to an interview script. The recorded interviews were also transcribed by an objective third party.

---

197   Merriam, 201.
198   Ibid, 207.

The Ethical Issues

Qualitative exploratory research presents unique ethical responsibilities.[199] The aims of this study were communicated to each potential interviewee as they were approached to be a continuing part of the study after completing the survey. I obtained permission from each participant to record each interview. Anonymity of the respondents was maintained by assigning a number to each of the participants, and by only using broad terms for their individual *statistical facts* (their names, home cities, church names, and seminaries were not used). Meanwhile, their broad distinctions (country, denomination, and theological affiliation) were used to give comparison data.

The goal of the interviewing portion of the research was to acquire a record of the attitudes and practices of the respondents through what they actually said, without any influence on my part.[200] The exploratory research required the recording of their responses. There was also a concern of the ethical nature of recording respondents' critical statements about any third parties. This concern is addressed by the anonymity of the respondents, and by the naming of only those public movements or figures whose ideas are already recorded in the public realm.

Part of the value of this study was the examination of the important debate surrounding the future of expository preaching. The recording of the respondents' critique of the ideas and attitudes surrounding this debate is vital. These personal attitudes represent part of the objective examination of this subject and are therefore ethically sound. Likewise, my theological reflection (Chapter 2) and final recommendations (Chapter 4) are offered as an ethical contribution to the ongoing study of this debate.

---

199   R. E. Stake, "Case Studies" in N.K. Denzin and Y.S. Lincoln (eds.), Handbook of Qualitative Research (Thousand Oaks, CA: SAGE Publishing, 1994), 244.
200   Patton, 354.

Survey Data Analysis

The surveys (Appendix A) provided rich data and insights into the attitudes and practices of these postmodern preachers. I randomly distributed the surveys to emergent church associations around the world, primarily through the Internet. Completed surveys were collected over a period of two years. From these survey respondents, I chose ten representative subjects on a random basis for further study. I created profiles of each subject for comparison data, and I did statistical analysis to compare these subject representatives.

Five denominations were represented among the ten interview subjects (figure 8a). They were Baptist (4), Lutheran (3), Vineyard (1), Brethren (1), and Independent (1). This was a good representative cross section of evangelical church denominations. These churches represent conservative, liberal, and charismatic traditions, liturgical and free worship service styles, episcopal and independent governance, Calvinist and Arminian theologies, as well as clergy and lay-centered leadership structures.

Four nationalities were represented: New Zealand (4), Canada (2), the United States (3), and England (1). This suited the goal of the exploration, as this was a study of preaching within the context of Western postmodern culture. The emergent church has no centralized organization, but each of these countries has national and regional organizations that are involved in the international emergent conversation.

Figure 8a
Statistical Chart of Ten Survey Responses
Respondent's Church Information

R	Affiliation	Nationality	Church Size	Average Age	Yrs Meeting
R1	Baptist	New Zealand	150-499	21-25	11-15
R2	Independent	Canada	30-99	16-20	1-5
R3	Lutheran	United States	100-149	16-20	11-15
R4	Brethren	Canada	501-1000	21-25	6-10
R5	Baptist	New Zealand	30-99	16-20	1-5
R6	Baptist	New Zealand	30-99	26-30	6-10
R7	Vineyard	England	150-499	21-25	6-10
R8	Lutheran	United States	100-149	16-20	6-10
R9	Baptist	New Zealand	30-99	31-35	6-10
R10	Lutheran	United States	30-99	10-15	1-5

The average church size of the ten respondent churches was 190 attendees. Only one church had over five hundred attendees, while seven churches averaged fewer than 150. Apart from a few exceptions, these emergent churches tend to be small gatherings.[201] These small numbers, for the vast majority of these emergent churches, may limit their influence upon the larger Western church scene. Only time will reveal how deep and lasting the impact of this non-movement conversational association will be. The average age of church attendees was 21.5. Only one respondent church's average age of attendees was over thirty, while another one averaged ages ten

---

201   Exceptions to the small emergent church rule would include Solomon's Porch in Minneapolis, Minnesota pastored by Doug Pagitt, and The Meeting House in Oakville, Ontario pastored by Bruxy Cavey.

to fifteen. This suggests that the emergent church may be primarily an age-specific phenomenon.

Figure 8b
Statistical Chart of Ten Survey Responses
Respondent's Church Service Information

R	Singing	Annnmnts	Preaching	Prayer	Reading	Other
R1	30	5	30	10		15
R2	30	5	30	5	5-10	5
R3	18	2	15	6	5	10
R4	45	15	35	5	5	15
R5	0	10	0	10	10	30
R6	0	5	18	10	2	25
R7	15	5	30	5	5	20
R8	15	5	20	5	5	0
R9	20	5	20	5	5	5
R10	15	0	20	15	5	25

During a typical weekly meeting (figure 8b), the respondent churches spent an average of 19.5 minutes singing, 5.7 minutes doing announcements, 21.8 minutes listening to a sermon, 7.6 minutes praying, 5.9 minutes reading biblical texts, and 15.5 minutes engaging in other activities ranging from sacraments and learning activities to questions and discussion time. In four cases, the sermon was shorter than another single aspect of the weekly church service. The average length of services was seventy-six minutes.

These leaders seem to see preaching as relevant and necessary, but the average time spent in sermon preparation among the ten respondents was only 9.7 hours, with some spending as little as one to five hours at the exegetical process. There is also a relatively low level of commitment to exegeting the biblical texts in their original languages. Some claim habits of regular attention to engaging Greek or Hebrew tools, though some made disparaging comments about doing so, and most confessed reliance on secondary sources as their primary means for biblical interpretation.

Figure 8c
Statistical Chart of Ten Survey Responses
Respondent's Personal Information

R	Age	Yrs Full Time	Education	Sermon Prep
R1	35-40	6-10	grad degree / sem.	8 hrs.
R2	26-30	1-5	some grad	11 hrs.
R3	40+	20+	post grad degree	6-10 hrs.
R4	31-35	11-15	grad degree	11-15 hrs.
R5	40+	20+	grad degree	10 hrs.
R6	31-35	6-10	post grad degree	1-5 hrs.
R7	31-35	1-5	post grad degree	1-5 hrs.
R8	40+	16-20	sem. training	11-15 hrs.
R9	26-30	1-5	grad degree	16-20 hrs.
R10	35-40	1-5	grad degree / sem.	10 hrs.

The representative subjects consisted of one woman (R10) and nine men (figure 8c). Their average age was 35.7. The average age of the church leaders was more than ten years older than that of the attendees. These church leaders had been in full-time ministry for an average of 10.3 years. This is very close to the average age of the churches themselves. This would suggest that their current churches make up the bulk of these leaders' ministry experience. The average years these churches had been meeting was 7.5. This may not be enough time to evaluate any lasting success in these churches surviving. Some of these churches may not exist in the near future. Again, only time will tell if they can sustain the transition from young start-ups focused almost exclusively on young people, to established, mature faith communities.

The average level of education for these emergent church leaders was a graduate degree, with no respondent having less than some graduate level education, and three having doctoral degrees. These leaders are highly educated individuals, though only four representative subjects had any seminary training. This suggests that secular education may be more highly valued than formal religious training.

Figure 8d
Statistical Chart of Ten Survey Responses
Respondent's Gifting Information

R	Gifts
R1	NA
R2	communication, inspiration, vision, direction, encouragement, empowerment
R3	worship, preaching, teaching, pastoral care, writing
R4	leadership, teaching, encouragement, music, vision, discernment, prophet
R5	communication, thinking
R6	communication, creativity, entrepreneur
R7	mentoring, training, min. to poor, catechism of new believers
R8	preaching, evangelism, hospitality
R9	communication, encouragement, motivating, training
R10	imagination, vision, planning, implementation, courage, passion

Only two respondents (R3 and R8) recorded "preaching" as one of their "leadership gifts" (figure 8d). The "leadership gift" word most repeated was "communication." Four subjects claimed this one. This may be a more postmodern way of describing the preaching act. Other words for claimed "leadership gifts" recorded by the subjects, which may also relate to public verbal ministry, were "teaching," "training," "direction," "motivating," "inspiration," "evangelism," "prophesy," and "encouragement." They may disparage traditional words for—and forms of—"preaching," but these representative leaders are committed to leading their people through verbal discourse, proclamation, and attention to the Scriptures.

When asked to describe what they had been preaching over the last twelve to eighteen months, most respondents described that they preached topically. Four stated their habit of using the liturgical lectionary. Only two respondents described that they taught through Bible texts systematically over a series of weeks as their regular practice. R2 stated, "I preached through the Gospel of John and now I am preaching through Acts.... I wanted to give our congregation an understanding of the life of Christ and life in the Holy Spirit. I am a big fan of exegetical preaching." R4 said, "It was a leadership decision ... we are slowly getting through the Bible. These books were our last stop.... After Luke, I don't know.... but guaranteed more Bible."

Many of the respondents described creative ways that they are attempting to have their people engage with biblical themes. R1 stated,

> We like to include symbolic responses as part of our worship, perhaps burning paper, or piling rocks on top of each other. For example, last week in a service looking at how we respond to God, we spent probably 20 minutes, where there was communion served, people could go into a corner and hold ice in their hands while they prayed prayers of confession, or put pieces of burning rock ... on a large block of ice (to symbolize their desire to make a difference in "heating the world").

R6 said his future plans for preaching included using "the New Zealand greatest songs of all time as my preaching text." R7 was planning "a series on being community, based on St. Benedict's rule of faith." R5 described his church service:

> The program is one hour long and varies enormously week to week. We don't sing, don't preach—always spend time in Scripture reading and prayer (one way or another), usually have music/video (often secular, reframed) and announcements. The preaching slot is taken up with discovery activities.

When asked what life events, ministry experiences, or people had been their greatest ministry influences, the respondents had a variety of answers. Some referred to their involvement with organizations they had worked with before their church experience: "with heroin addicts for four years" (R1), "Young Life" (R2), "the Lutheran World Federation, the World Council of Churches, [and] ecumenical campus ministry" (R3), "Willow Creek in Chicago" (R8), and "Habitat For Humanity" (R10). Some respondents named specific individuals: "[Karl] Marx … [Dietrich] Bonhoeffer, [Jacques] Ellul, [Lesslie] Newbigin, Jim Wallis, [Eugene] Peterson, and [Brian] McLaren" (R4), "Brian McLaren" and "Todd Hunter" (R7), and "Dave Andrews" (R9). Some mentioned secular experiences: "a background as a computer consultant/manager" (R1), "spending the amount of time I have in and around Whistler" (R2), "my friends not in church" (R6), and "the Waiter's Union in Brisbane, Australia" (R9). Some mentioned international experiences: "I worked in Hong Kong" (R1), "travel in Latin America, Europe, Africa" (R3), and "growing up in an overseas environment gave me cross-cultural understandings" (R6). A few mentioned their families: "knowing [his wife]" (R2) and "my own kids" (R8). Only R2 and R9 mentioned formal theological education. R10 mentioned her "personal trauma." There was no one person, thing, or experience that was common to even a few of these leaders.

When asked to record what (if any) changes they would like to see in their churches over the next five years, five respondents shared concerns for outreach: "the fundamental question that our church is wrestling with … is how best to do mission in [our country]" (R1), "I want to see more people come to know Christ" (R2), "more penetrating engagement" (R4), "I'd like to see the new folks re-energize the others with a heart for evangelism and outreach" (R8), and "more Xers coming to faith" (R6).

Though only one respondent made comments about social issues, "develop our ministry to the poor further" (R7), there were several who commented about engaging their culture. R4 wanted to "deepen community." R9 wanted to be "more holistic beyond our gathered community" and he wanted "less of a Sunday-service orientation to the life of the church community." R10 said she wanted to see "additional satellite ministries led by participants in the community." They are very concerned that the Church is relevant to their contemporaries. R1 said,

> Another [fundamental thing our church is wrestling with] is how best to be church. I suspect this involves some serious untangling of tradition to weave a system of being that makes disciples who are unashamed to engage with the culture around them in a positive and non-retreatist way. I don't have a clear template to achieve this, but have confidence that if we as a community wrestle with this stuff, we will find ourselves changing both our images of how we are church and the mechanics of how we "do church."

Several respondents pointed to changes they would like to make in their worship service: "I would like to see our services be far more led by the congregation than by the leadership. When filling this out I realized that prayer is not a big part of our services at all; I would like to see that change" (R2); "[I would like to] continue to use a variety of liturgical resources" (R3); "Maybe equipping even more people to teach … more effective beauty" (R4); and "our church seems to be leaning toward 'comfort' with those who have worshipped here for a number of years" (R8). R3's greatest concern for change over the next five years was "architectural changes to our worship space from a traditional, linear arrangement of pews to one more in the round."

In regard to Spiritual formation, only three respondents mentioned a desire for greater Bible teaching. R2 wanted "to see opportunities for more people to be equipped to study their Bibles on their own time … stronger cell groups and discipleship groups [and that he] would like to become a better teacher and free up more time to spend on preparation." R4 wanted to "sharpen orthodoxy." And

R7 wanted to better "mentor, train, and release ... young leaders into ministry [and to develop a] catechism of new believers."

These representative emergent leaders were all very aware of the *ethos* of their contemporary culture. They shared a deep concern to see their churches be relevant and accessible to the people (especially young people) of their communities. They demonstrated their concern for the development of a great understanding of authentic Christianity in the postmodern West through their willingness to participate in this study.

In the following excerpts from the surveys, each of the respondents described his or her typical sermon preparation:

R1:

> Depends on the topic of course. I read anything I can, talk to anyone who seems to be an expert or be wrestling with the same topics. I visit what websites are helpful, check out the local university library. Prayer makes it in there as well somehow.

R2:

> I read the text devotionally. I pray. I attempt to understand the message of the text for myself and determine how I think I can best communicate it. I do word studies and look at similar texts/passages. I check commentaries and then I structure a sermon that I think best communicates what the passage is teaching. I pray and speak it.

R3:

> Read the text many times over several days. Bible study. Read commentaries. Think. Reflect. Pray. Let the ideas and themes "simmer" for a while. Draft the notes Saturday. Get up early Sunday morning and finalize the notes. Be able to preach from notes rather than reading from a manuscript. I've

sometimes participated in pericope study groups, but haven't for several years.

R4:

Prayer, Scripture reading, study, pondering, a walk on the beach, consulting commentaries and other secondary sources, outline, conversation (Wednesday afternoon), writing text.

R5:

Find the main points of the passage. List the applications. Make the applications the points— illustrate from situations people actually find themselves in.

R6:

Time wise, I try to engage with a Bible text through commentaries on the Tuesday. Then I put it out on the Internet to the community over the week to invite community feedback and questions. I sit with the application/connectivity over the week and do a number of drafts over the weekend. It's like giving birth—it's just a struggle, but something coheres. It's a very creative, intuitive process.

R7:

When doing a series I would research for 2–3 hours to gather materials and resources, then do an outline. Weekly, about 2 hours a week preparation. Handouts with notes and Bible verses are made for every talk. I see myself as a teacher, trying to use the teaching resources of the best people I can find to teach my church.

R8:

Read the text, and let that filter through my thinking for a couple of days. I use *Homiletics Online* for stories and commentary. All of this "stewing" takes about 4–5 days.

Two days before the sermon is due I begin writing. I know that at some point I need to "STAGE" this work (actually stand on the preaching platform [stage] and preach it). So, I have several components to the sermon:

Story: Some "hook" to increase interest in text.
Text: Brief teaching about the context.
What did it mean then?
Application: What does this mean for us now?
Life Lessons, etc.
Gospel: What's the Good News in this for us?
Ending: Creative, compelling, Challenging Call.

R9:

[I] start with a text, issue, or proposition. Some kind of dialogue with God. Read the passage a bit in different translations, etc. Get a handle on the unit of thought I'm wanting to study in the passage. Identify what's going on in the passage—the people, what they're up to, etc, who, what, where, when, etc. Look at some significant word stuff that may be showing itself—action words, repeated words, etc. See if there's anything jumping out at me that's doing it for me.... Study some of the significant words.... Create some sort of summary of the passage. I like to sit on it for a while now—leave it overnight, or for a day—just to let it mull over in my mind, hopefully God/Spirit will be interacting with me on different levels.... Create a kind of outline/structure. Look at some commentaries (2 or 3). (I was taught NEVER to start with the commentaries!). Start writing what I'm going to say.

R10:

> Ponder topic, explore music (we use a lot of secular music), Scripture reading and identification of text, check the lectionary, research (books, Internet, magazines), prepare a draft, rewrite, practice.

Only R1 does not mention the Bible as a primary source. The others call it the "text" (R2, R3, R8, R9, and R10), the "Scripture" (R4 and R10), the "Bible" (R3, R6, R7), and the "passage" (R2 and R5). They used very different approaches to developing their sermons, but each demonstrated concern to proclaim the *logos* of God's Word to their contemporary *ethos* with authentic *pathos*.

The Interview Data Analysis

The exploratory method of the initial surveys provided material for follow-up interviews. I interviewed each of the ten representative subjects using the same interview question design (Appendix B). The interviews focused on the individual attitudes towards and practices of the sermonic process among the ten respondents. I recorded and analyzed their responses to better explore the insights and experiences of these emergent church leaders, who are directly involved in attempts to successfully engage postmodern church attendees with biblical messages. The individual interviews provided for an open dialogue with these church leaders, allowing them to articulate their insights and observations in response to a casual conversation with me to explore how these emerging church leaders understand the postmodern context and its influence on their preaching.

These interviews were then transcribed for further exploration. With such diversity represented by these subjects, I looked for common elements in their responses. After careful analysis of the ten interviews, using the framework of the three elements of the rhetorical paradigm—*ethos, pathos* and *logos* discussed in Chapter 3—nine themes emerged as primary issues for further study. I detected three themes for each rhetorical element. These themes were Community, Activity, Sensuality, Humility, Irreverence,[202] Inquiry, Relevancy, Necessity, and Text. Each of these nine primary themes falls under one of the three elements of the rhetorical paradigm. Community, Activity, and Sensuality are subjects of *ethos*. Humility, Inquiry, and Irreverence are subjects of *pathos*. Relevancy, Necessity, and Text are subjects of *logos*. The following is an examination of each of these themes, in turn, through the responses of each of the ten respondent conveyors.

The Ethos of Postmodern Preaching

A. Community

The *ethos* of the sermon is the perceived ability of the conveyor of the *logos* to connect with the language, history, and culture of the contemporary context. Each of the respondents articulated the importance of the *ethos* of postmodern preaching being couched in and shaped by the community within which the message is proclaimed. R1 articulated an attitude toward the sermonic process that involves a cyclical journey for the preacher and his audience:

> Preaching is supposed to be a cycle, I think. You do your hard work, you do your hard praying, then you go out and say your thing. But it doesn't stop there. It goes into a community who picks it apart … it becomes a journey. And then we try to bring that into the service a bit.… [It's] probably more of a community understanding than a written one. And [it] is about creating a type of community.

Common among these postmodern preachers is little separation between the preacher and his community. Even the message itself

---

202   The word "irreverent" was first suggested to me by Randy Hein, pastor of The Place in Victoria, British Columbia.

is shaped by a regular and authentic interaction of the preacher with his faith community. Not only is the message shaped by the consideration of the receptor community, some preachers are practicing an open invitation to their community to participate in the very exegesis of the text the message is based on. R3 stated that he regularly has a Bible study on Tuesday mornings to bring people from the congregation together to look at the text to be read the following Sunday at worship. He says, "We would read the text together and do a Bible study on that text [asking] how the text spoke to these participants both in their own lives and in their own cultural settings." This becomes a concrete, open invitation to the community to be actively involved in helping to shape the very proclamation of the Bible teaching. R6 commented,

> I would send out every Tuesday to anyone who wanted it, by e-mail, the text for the day. The text for the week or a quote or a question or something in relation to what I was going to preach. We would have an Internet discussion group. Basically, we would talk about that text. That was like me tossing the Scriptures into the midst of the community. They would gnaw them together. There was a sense that as I, the preacher, came to the text I was coming to it aware of the community's questions, aware of their encouragement, their disagreements, their anger or whatever it was in relation to the text.

R7 describes how this process of communal exegesis sometimes takes place right in the service during the usual preaching time:

> Once a month we do an exercise where we read a biblical story. We do it in community. We read it from the Message or the NIV. We get someone to read it in church. We get people to close their eyes and listen to it again.… It is a more participatory learning experience. The other thing that happens

is I end up learning things from people.... Some of the observations they have are just astounding. It is a two-way learning experience. I found myself sometimes going, "Gosh, I have never noticed that." We get a high level of participation when we do that.

R6 described the similar attempts he has used to help the community engage with the interpretation of the biblical texts, saying, "I think one of the key parts of contemporary preaching/ postmodern preaching is that there is a conversation around the Scripture that is owned by the community." He believes the vital task of the preacher is "to engage the community around the text." He shared some of the things he did at his church to "empower the community to have a sense of engagement with that biblical text." These included "telling a story in relation to the text" or inviting people to offer input "into the shape of the sermon or reflecting beforehand on the Bible text." He does this through what they call "the communal text." He puts it out on the Internet to the community over the week "to invite community feedback and questions." He says, "Someone might articulate something really well or they might raise a really good question. Often I would bring those into my sermon. There was a sense that I was engaging with respect to the conversation from the congregation, the community."

When asked if he had ever had his mind changed regarding the meaning of a text because of the communal interaction with the preacher and the text, R6 said, "Yes, all the time." He commented,

[I am] changed but also challenged in new ways or taken in new directions for my sermon. Often I would do the commentary stuff on the Tuesday and then think, the text may mean this by the end of the week. I would give it to the community and think this is the issue the text is wrestling with. If I want to be faithful to the text and community then I will have to discuss this as well. I am the servant of the community, and therefore, the text needs to speak to the issues, the questions, the encouragement that the community has around this text.

R8 is involved in communal interpretation of biblical texts every week, as he is involved in creating teaching resources for his church's many ministries, as well as those of other churches. He describes this communal process: "We sit around the table [and] I just lay this all out and then they push back.… We spend an hour and we just, you know, toss this potato back and forth. I'm taking notes, they're all taking notes." R4 recognized that this commitment to connecting the sermon to one's community is not easy. He said, "That is effective but difficult preaching.… When we teach God's Word we ought to inspire people. I think before we have any authority and before we can inspire we have to identify with our community."

When asked to describe his typical sermon preparation, R4 included "prayer, Scripture reading, study, pondering, a walk on the beach, consulting commentaries, other secondary sources," as well as "outline, conversation and a Wednesday afternoon meeting." For this emergent preacher, sermon preparation involves not only exegetical study, but interaction with the community he preaches to. He added,

> There is a tone and a demeanor that sometimes surrounds the word "expository." It says that the scholar sits down and uses scholarship to arrive at the truth. While I think that homework is really, really significant and important, I understand that I am preaching in the context of community.… I have the legacy of the saints behind me. The reality of the saints is in front of me, surrounding me in community.

When asked what he would say is the most important task of a leader in the "emergent church," R4 replied, "To listen: to listen to Scripture, to listen through prayer, to listen to your culture and to listen to your community. Within that listening to attempt to understand what it is that God is saying, what it is your community is saying, and what it is your culture is saying. Then lead accordingly."

R2 confessed that one of the most significant influences on his preaching was a weekend retreat where four Bible teachers taught 2 Timothy systematically in communal concert. He said, "I think my number one experience was that weekend seeing God's word preached by a number of different people but it still being God's word." He lamented his own inability to connect his preaching more readily to his own community when he said,

> The one thing that I really felt like I missed is that it did not touch down in the lives of the people who were hearing it. How does that apply to what I am going to do tomorrow? How does that apply to how I am going to speak to my roommates? I fell into the trap of sometimes using words like "repent" or "blessing." These are words that are full of such great meaning, but what does it mean that I will walk away from here and bless my friends?

R5 described how the priority of community determined the very structure of his church service. He started out thinking that they would always have a traditional sermon during the service, but "within a few weeks [they] realized that whole way of one person being an imparter and the rest being receivers was clashing with the whole mindset of what we were trying to do." He continued,

> People were coming along because they felt that we were on a spiritual journey. They wanted to share that journey with other people. It was more a matter of trying to have a format where we could discover together, rather than have one person at the front imparting truths that others would receive.

R7 likewise articulated how he sees preaching as a journey the church community takes together to help him "make sense of where we are at and where I am at." He said,

> This whole postmodern thing has been helpful to us in realizing that interpretation occurs in community. Biblical preaching is not about me telling you the pure meaning of the text. It is about a community bringing and retelling the text together so that the story becomes alive and part of who we are.

R10 observed that the understanding of this communal aspect of the emergent church is the most important task of emergent preachers. She said, "I think the most important task is to allow God to be God and to join people on their journey rather than proclaiming their own way as the end of the journey, and knowing that they are helping you along as well." Likewise, R9 commented, "I think community is important. Relationship is more important than lots of relationships.… I like to think of members as being a participation thing. Hopefully being part of the faith community then a commitment will come."

R10 described how her church is "building" their church and Bible preaching from within a specific community. She said, "There's still, you know, two-thirds of the community that are not churched or who have specifically left the church because they've been hurt; [our church] is specifically about trying to reach those people who have been alienated from the church, hurt by the church, or had no exposure to the church." She said they do this by building community through many relational activities, much like the early Church. The Bible teaching is done, then, in the context of these relational activities. She explained,

> We have the Sunday night gathering, which is where we have worship and then a meal and then chat.… We have the communion meal, but then we have a full dinner, and then we have our chat time, where

we talk about some topic that we've decided ahead of time … I've been very intentional about trying to find multiple ways in which to go to people where they are and allow people different places to connect so they can feel comfortable and perhaps move into the larger community but at their pace.

They also use the contemporary technology of the Internet to develop the community of their church. She thinks the Internet is "an important realm." She thinks it allows her community "to enter into a lot of different communities that [they] otherwise would not have the opportunity to explore." She said, "E-mail is our number one way of communicating with extended groups." They have started a chat site online. She said a large number of people log on to the site. She has posted her sermons there and "now there are a lot of people that are connected with the community virtually."

R9 talked about how the book *The Celtic Way of Evangelism,* by George C. Hunter III, connected with his ideas of church community in a postmodern setting. He said,

[Hunter] talks about how they kind of invited people into this community and belonging…. They did not have to make a commitment. They had to weigh whether they wanted to make a commitment or not. Often people would kind of discover that they did believe in God after a time of being included in the community. They would commit and eventually be part of a formal baptism or something like that.

All ten of these emergent church leaders described the importance of the primary issue of Community in the practice of exposing their congregations to the Word of God. Because of the unique pluralistic sensitivities of the postmodern worldview (figure 1), the emergent Christian leader must rely on his faith community to help the *logos* to be contextualized within the *ethos* of his congregation, from the first steps of exegesis on to the final steps of application.

B. Activity

Each of the respondents mentioned aspects of the importance of Activity in their preaching. There is a need for postmoderns to see the direct applications of preaching in their real life *ethos*, and to actively be involved in the sermonic event. R7 simply states that his preaching "is very participatory." R2 said he always asks, "How do I best live out what I have learned?"

R5 articulated the way that the postmodern paradigm challenges the rationalism of the modernist worldview, saying, "I guess we are also using the concept that Christian growth is not necessarily equated with knowledge. It is more how we live out the faith. Rather than being a whole thing of trying to know more, we are trying to better be Christian people." R1 explained how he has had to create a way for his congregation's experience to be more active during their weekly service: "One of the things we've done is try to introduce discussion in the middle of it." Likewise, R8 did the "hard" work of creating an active ministry out of his church to help the young people actively apply their faith by engaging with their world. He explained,

> We would take a large group of high school kids on a tour. My partner and I would write a musical every year and create a band, actors, and stuff. The largest group we had was somewhere over 320 kids. We put them on eight buses and went to, that year I think we went to San Diego. Every year we have done this and that particular track or those kids that go on that trip and prepare for that trip.... Yeah, you know, boy it's hard.

R10 told how she uses many different activities to connect the message to the real lives of her congregation members. "We use meditation or chants after our message time, some kind of contemplation, a lot of times drawing on Christian mysticism.... We always end with the communion feast." R3 described where he sees expository preaching being abandoned because it may tend to be passive entertainment and not active enough for postmoderns: "I guess one place of abandonment would be in some of the churches that are shifting towards a more entertainment style of preaching." He mentioned Willow Creek as an example. R4 mentioned that he sees a problem with the preacher-as-uninvolved-expert who is not actively involved with his congregation, even in exegesis. He said,

> I know that there are other factors that are involved in preaching than simply scholars sitting down and closing themselves in a room—working it all out until he comes to the truth ... like Descartes in his room during the Enlightenment and coming to it on his own.

This is a particularly postmodern complaint against the rationalism of the modernist approach to preaching. The modernist preacher is perceived to be an "ivory tower"-dwelling academic who descends weekly to dispense dogmatic doctrines that are automatically authoritative and must be ascended to intellectually and obeyed morally. There is a common revulsion on the part of the postmodern audience towards any kind of imposed authority. Postmoderns are "unanchored and responsible to no one" (figure 1) and they uniquely grasp truth, not rationally, but actively. It must be lived to be understood. R6 says,

> [If] the Bible is removed from the world, that, to me, makes the travesty of the Bible because it is a deeply committed book in terms of engaging in the world that we live in. By being biblical preachers we have to engage with the world that we are part of. Why? Because the Bible is engaged with the world that it is a part of.

R9 links membership in the faith community itself to active participation. He talked about "Baptist churches who traditionally have closed membership," complaining about having "to be baptized before you could be a member." He "[does] not like that idea." He surmised that "membership is symbolized by our participation in the community, especially if someone is doing anything in the community at all.… It is a participation thing like in a family. You have to participate to be a part of it."

Each of the ten respondents identified the primary issue of Activity as an important part of the *ethos* of each of their congregations. As is the case of every preacher in every age, these postmodern preachers suggested that the emergent biblical expositor must create ways for his message to actively engage the real lives of his congregation. Because Western culture is so profoundly secularized, the postmodern person needs to see that the sermon actually "works" outside of the church setting, out in the "real world." They suggest that the message also must move from being predominantly theoretical and verbal to being more practical and visual.

C. Sensuality

Each of the respondents also identified issues related to engaging the *ethos* of the whole person more readily through their full physical sensuality. This involves actually engaging as many of the five human senses of the members of the congregation as possible. R7 described how his church does an exercise to engage people's senses in the Bible story. He said,

> We get someone to read it in church. We get people to close their eyes and listen to it again. We then ask people to shout out words, images, and smells.… If we retell this story and we imagine ourselves in it, what do we notice? One that we did recently was the story of when people come to the tomb. Peter notices the linen that Jesus was wrapped in. She looked in and noticed the angel. We read that story and we got people to say what they saw. Some people

said, "Peter was really hot and sweaty." Someone said, "It is really bright." Someone said something about the different smells that they have. It is very participatory. Many people get involved in that.

R1 described a communion service that involved a unique sensual experience of the ancient sacrament in a local pub: "That was sort of playing with the stuff of our world and bringing it into how you try and do church." R5 described a physical activity that engaged his congregation's five senses in an Easter experience. Using a hammer and nails to make their own crosses, "they nailed the things that they thought God was not very happy about to the crosses." R8 also described using multimedia to engage all five senses of his congregation:

> We are highly visual. We have screens, which sort of add some dimension. This weekend I am sort of going three-dimensional. We are going to try to use some images from the *Passion of the Christ* movie. I am also going to try to bring in about twenty plastic gasoline cans and pile them up and stand in the middle of them with a lit lighter. We are dealing with the temptation of Christ. And then on the other side of the sanctuary, with a platform, I am going to literally haul in a big wooden cross … it's also got to be engaging and visual.

R6 described seeing this connection to the physical world in which people live as a vital part of helping people engage the text of Scripture. He cited the Apostle Paul as a great example of someone wanting to communicate to his contemporary audience. He suggests that Paul "was aware of the world that he lived in. [It] became part of his horizon." He suggests that the preaching of the Scriptures "always fit in their context." He said, "We have to preach them as context. They were ultimately the communication of God's truth; therefore, to be a biblical preacher today we also must be committed to the communication of God's truth in our context." R6 continued, focusing on one scene from the Gospels where the disciples did not fully understand Jesus' preaching until they had experienced a fully physical, sensual engagement of all their five senses:

> The biblical model for that would be the Emmaus Road story. Jesus preaches and they do not get it as they walk down the road. He offers the law and the prophets and his new understanding of the exposition of the text. It is not until they are gathered around the table, breaking bread, that Jesus is revealed. It seems to me there that the text is saying you must combine exposition with community. The task of the preacher is to engage the community around the text.

R4 also invoked Jesus' teaching method to endorse this postmodern attraction to sensual experience: "In Jesus' method of communication he predominantly told stories and asked questions. We predominantly write essays that we preach to people and give answers." R4 commented that he believes Christians are "called to embrace mystery in the Christian tradition." He said, "I believe modernism tried to deconstruct mystery. I think during the last five hundred years we have more doctrinal books on understanding the Trinity than experiencing the Trinity. Sometimes I am called to enter into faith and embrace mysteries, which can be logically polarizing at times."

Jesus told colorful stories that engaged the imaginations of his hearers. It is this attention to excellent storytelling that most of the respondents identified as the best way to engage the fully sensual *ethos* of their postmodern congregations. Good storytelling can engage all five senses through the imagination. R7 said,

> I think primarily we are creatures of story. We live our lives in story. We remember things as stories and memories. Real biblical preaching would be

storytelling just as our family history. These are our family poetry books. These are our family photo albums, snapshots, blogs, journals, you name it. These are the things that collectively give us a window into retelling how God has interacted with His people over time. We have church history. We need to tell our story. We need to locate ourselves in that story. I think biblical preaching would do that—to furnish our imaginations and retell the story.

R8 concurred, adding a critique of traditional lecture-style sermons, saying, "The whole idea of story and the biblical story is so important. In preaching, what works more and more is not a 'talking head,' but how your story and my story connect with God's story." R9 confesses, "I am not a great storyteller." But he believes that a good storyteller "can communicate something of the text. They do not just tell a story, but they have done some research. They know details behind that story. The way that they communicate to the people listening can be done really powerfully." He believes in "using multiple mediums" because they are "traditionally what preaching is." He said he thinks postmodern preachers "need to experiment and try to use images, dance, and music, which brings us to the worship side of things."

Likewise, R1 said he thought the work of creating this imaginative space was a vital part of connecting the *logos* of God's Word to the people in the postmodern *ethos*. He said, "We go out of our way to try and create a space, even if it's a mental one, into which people can play and think. Everybody has to provide their own imagination to make that." R2 pointed out the imagery of the Bible, which engages all five senses:

> Jesus spoke about the "Day of the Lord" kind of thing and what that looks like. It talks about the sky turning dark and stuff like that. We are looking at a passage right now in chapter eight and nine where

the trumpet is being blown and the bride is coming
down. I use a lot of Old Testament stuff as well. I
have been doing a lot of Exodus studies, Isaiah kind
of stuff, and trying to find out what that imagery
means in the context here.

R8 described what he believes was "the best" fully sensual
experience sermon he had witnessed, when a preacher gave a message
on the "Day of Atonement":

[The preacher] brought a goat out on stage. He had
the high priest in complete, full, authentic robes. He
described that robe. He described what was going
on and why the need for the goat and everything.
At the end of forty-five minutes, when the priest
finally sits down after the goat has left the building
… four thousand people erupted out of their chairs.
It was complete Easter morning pandemonium joy
for about five minutes. It was unbelievable. And
so, he did his exegesis. He taught right out of the
text and we will never have a doubt or a question
about the Day of Atonement and what was going
on there again.

R8 was articulating the high value that the postmodern culture
places on communication that engages all five human senses. R10
also uses the sensorial experiences of her contemporary *ethos* to
engage her congregation. She commented, "Stories, parables, visual
aids are always wonderful." She said she thinks it's important that
"we explore multiple means of communication and that we be able to
break out of the strictly spoken linear 'Here's the five points,' to look
at creative ways and stories and examples and means." She said that
she uses "a lot of video clips and music, those kinds of things."

Likewise, R1 said, "I'm very interested in images and symbols …
it's who I am." These postmodern preachers are not only sensitive to
the sensual *ethos* of their audience, but they, themselves, are steeped

in the postmodern world. R7 agreed with the idea of better use of imagery for this generation, saying, "We need to use imagery." R6 mentioned how Mitchell Stephens' book *The Rise of the Image, the Fall of the Word* has shaped his thinking about image-based preaching. It has also shaped his preaching:

> Often my sermon will be mostly one image that I will play with.… I am not really preaching three points. I am preaching one image. I would like to leave people with one word or one mental picture, and offer a range of perspectives on that. It is almost like, what is the one image that holds or is faithful through this text and to my community? How can I play with it? Play, not in a child's play idea, but play in terms of opening people's imaginations through this so that they go away with more to think about.

R3 said that in his preaching he is trying to "deepen their faith, awaken their faith, deepen their sense of discipleship, and broaden their sense of how the Gospel is broad in the world. The spirit of God is working in places where they may not have first planned." R6 commented, "If [expository preaching] is used, it has to be used in a more image-based experiential and communal sort of way." He said he believes that it does not have a place "if it is reducing one person to a rational standing over the text." But it does have a place "if it opens the community up [and allows] for them to engage with the fullness of Scripture." He said,

> Let's have the text but let's not have it bound up with the foundational, rational, logical approach to the community.… To me the Bible is so important that it has to be accessed in a whole lot of ways. Along with Bible preaching on Sundays, we will offer art and geology. We read Revelation and then

we invite musicians in to express that in music. That is another way of engaging the text.

All ten of these emergent church leaders described the importance of the primary issue of Sensuality in the practice of exposing their congregations to the Word of God. These postmodern preachers believe that the emergent biblical expositor must engage the full sensorial experience of his congregation to help the *logos* be contextualized within his contemporary *ethos*. This is true, from the first stages of capturing the imagination and interest of the congregation in the exegesis of the text, to the final steps of applying God's Word to their own life experience.

The Pathos of Postmodern Preaching

A. Humility

The *pathos* of the sermon is the ability of the speaker to connect with his audience. It is the perceived authenticity, authority, and integrity of the conveyor of the message. Each of the respondents identified aspects of the primary issue of Humility as a vital part of the authentic *pathos* of the emergent preacher. R4 commented, "I think scholarship has to be bathed in humility. It has to be bathed in prayer and in communal understanding." He said that he sees humble honesty as an important part of exposing the text of Scripture. He said,

> When you look at the text and you actually explore it, you are left with some real questions. You can preach a sermon that will justify those things away, or you can preach a sermon where, at the end of the day, you look to your congregation and say, "This is what the passage says. This is what I have explored and attempted to understand and grappled with, but at the end of the day, I do not know why some of

this is here." When you talk about honesty, I think that is where some of the honesty is. That is honesty with the text. When we exegete the text sometimes we are left honestly with questions. I think when we exegete our community we also have to approach it with a degree of honesty as to where people are at.

R5 agreed; he parodied what he sees as a typical modernist preacher saying, "Here are the questions raised by the passage, and I have studied it this week. Here are all the answers." He said he believes that some evangelical people like to leave church having heard answers they knew all along. In contrast, he said, "For the emerging congregation we are really not trying to do anything like that. We are raising the questions and leaving them with the question." He said, "The truth is not actually found in the message; it is found in the conversation." That is a big difference. He is saying that he believes this has an enormous impact on the way postmodern people will perceive the *pathos* of the preacher.

When asked what the most important task of a leader in the emergent church is, R8 was clear to point out that he believes it is this quality of humility, rather than academic status. He stated, "It is just honesty and a living, breathing faith in the leader." He said he believes that the *pathos* of the leader is seen through their evident "relationship with Jesus Christ." And he said, "It's got to have a heart beating and that's got to be the starting point." He contrasted this postmodern "feeling" emphasis with a modernist rational emphasis (figure 7), saying, "I've known people who are educated up the ying-yang and they cannot make a connection with the emerging culture. But I know people who don't have a lot of education but they are able to communicate … they have to have a passion to tell the story."

For each of these emergent leaders, humility meant moving the centrality off of the preacher as authority figure, and onto the person of Christ. R8 said, "I think it is way easy for me or any other preacher to make [myself] central and my own biases, my own needs or limitations or whatever that I bring to the text." He said he believes one must humbly confess this tendency and "keep Christ central.... Otherwise, I get me in there and it is not about me. It is really about Christ." R4 reflected on how this is a shift from a previous generation:

> I think there was probably a generation, maybe one or two generations ago, in which what was important was that the preacher had authority; positional authority. I think it was also important that the preacher inspired people. I do not want to say that those things do not exist today. I think authority is still important in the Church. The Scriptures, from my vantage point, are inspired texts and they ought to inspire us at times. They ought to challenge us. When we teach God's Word we ought to inspire people. I think before we have any authority and before we can inspire, we have to identify with our community.... I do not necessarily think my parents would have bought that themselves, being baby boomers. They do like an inspirational sermon. They like someone who has their life together to climb into the pulpit and to be very motivational in their approach to teaching Scriptures. That idea of just inspirational preaching that can give small, propositional statements. They can break it down to three points that they can carry home. I think for the emerging generation that can often be perceived as a trivialization of the truth.

R5 agreed, describing how some of the traditional, modernist ways of preaching are a deterrent to postmodern listeners. He said, "The didactic style of church presentation is a real barrier for the emerging church. It puts people into those who know and those who do not know." He offered his vision of a more humble approach, saying, "I think we have to recognize in the emerging congregation that we are people on a journey together. We respect each other's journey with God. We are all learners together. We find a way of learning together that does not put people in one person imparting and the other people receiving."

R4 described the humility he has in approaching his own exegetical study of the Scriptures: "I have friends who are various scholars in various institutions that I can consult [when] I do not understand this text." He said he asks them, "Can you help me understand the Greek or the Hebrew surrounding this?" Likewise, in humility, R2 simply said, "I lean on people who have gone before me a lot." R3 asks his congregants, "Okay, if you had to preach on this text this coming Sunday to our particular congregation, what would you say?"

This kind of humility is something of a postmodern reaction to what many of the respondents talked about in terms of "power." R5 said, "I do think it is all tied up with power." When working with seminary students, he said noticed that they had trouble coming into his church, because his approach to listening to the Bible "strips the power away." He observed that when "everybody has an equal say in [Bible interpretation], and the [modernist] role of one man being the great dispenser of truth, whom everybody has to look to is gone," some of the seminary students did not like it. He said, "We have a discussion or a discovery activity and [these seminary students] want to give everyone the answer. They are the authority."

There are gender issues here too. He observed that "women do not have so much trouble with it." He theorized, "I think guys, male theological students, have a lot of power issues involved. They do not like the idea that they do not have the answer above everyone else. They would not say that. I think there are underlying issues there. Why do they always have to have the last word?" Likewise, R6 related an experience of "power" in a sermon:

> I listened to someone preach this year and they spoke for an hour. All they did was explain the Bible text. They used a whole lot of big words to explain the Bible. The take-home message from that really was that the Bible is totally irrelevant. The only way you could understand it is if I talk for an

hour and explain it to you with big words that I have found in my Bible commentary. What that is actually doing is disempowering people, ordinary everyday people, from preaching the Bible.... [It is about] empowerment in the sense that [it] is ... one privileged voice. That voice goes to seminary and that voice gets taught about the Bible.... I think about that horrible sermon that I saw. It was one man talking on and on. The way he talked said he was the expert, and the text was talked about in a way so that you could actually not understand it unless the experts told you what it was about.

This is a typical lament of postmodern thinkers. It is the extreme libertine reaction to premodernist institutional authority and modernist rational authority. The postmodern self is "over" all others and is ultimately free to make personal "choices," even on issues of "truth" according to the authority of personal preference (figure 1). These postmodern preachers are advocating a kind of humility in helping people hear the Word of God. R10 described a danger she sees in the traditional authority figure without humility, saying, "I think people have lost respect [for preachers] when they hold themselves up as something superhuman." She said she believes it is important that leaders "not use our congregation and our people as, at risk of abusing people, coming to them with our neediness." This is where she sees humility is needed in preaching. She said, "We also need to say, 'this is my best guess.' From what I have seen and from what I have experienced and from what I have read, this is what I think is true. I might be wrong. I would love to share with you what this means to me. I would love to hear from you what you have gone through and what you have experienced." R1 simply called these "superhuman" expectations "middle class prudery":

There's a lot of ... middle class prudery as opposed to discipleship.... I don't want to build a church of "shoulds." I think that's one of the legacies of

Christendom that has really hurt us. What I mean is that the very propositional style of preaching that has been popular is all about telling people what they should do. But actually I've got a whole bunch of people who already know what they should do. *I* already know what I should do! The issue is I don't. And, no offence, but if you come to me and you give me another twenty things to add to my hundred, do I walk away any better off? No! I walk away feeling more guilty because I've got another ten things on my list. It's gotten longer.

He offered ideas to combat this "prudery" with a kind of humility in preaching. One of the things he said he tries to do is to "introduce discussion in the middle of [it]." He also said he tries to "create things that will allow for multiple voices and multiple opinions." He said in his setting, "power really matters.... So, the kind of leader that [we] want is not somebody who's going to take control ... it is about creating community where you're not necessarily in power." Similarly, R9 said he thinks the very term "emergent" is antithetical to authentic humble *pathos* for the postmodern Church leader. He humbly remarked,

> I actually do not like the term "emergent church." I do not know what I would call it. "Emergent" makes me think "arrogant." Almost giving a finger to the Church as we knew it. I think the emergent church runs the risk of taking what we want from the past and going on ahead and not kind of acknowledging where our past has come from. If we look at the past and the history we will probably find a lot of emergent kind of churches that did not call themselves "emergent." I do not think this is a new thing. It is just a different way of being churched. I do not think the term "emergent church" reflects that well enough.

All of these emergent leaders talked about using good questions to help their congregations engage with God's Word. R7 confessed, "We made the mistake of swinging the other way from good teaching to 'please, do not ask me any more questions.' We try to moderate that more." For R10, this honest humility comes from her very being. She said, "I'm heavy on preaching grace and social justice. And I really enjoy liberation theology. And I think a lot of that comes certainly from a lot of my past experiences, both personally and in a work environment." She confessed to being a "survivor of domestic violence and a survivor of sexual abuse." She has worked as an executive director of Habitat for Humanity and has always had a strong passion for social justice. She said,

> We're reaching out to people who are homeless, who are unemployed, who are college students who don't have finances, who aren't used to going anyplace every Sunday and just really trying to figure out who we're forgetting and then making a point of being a presence there…. And especially as we do a lot of social justice things. I mean, you know, you pull up Jesus, and guess what? There's social justice.

All ten of these emergent church leaders described the importance of the primary issue of Humility in the practice of exposing their congregations to the Word of God. The emergent biblical expositor must have the discernable *pathos* of humility to have the kind of perceived authenticity, authority, and integrity that wins a hearing for the *logos* in this postmodern *ethos*.

B. Inquiry

Each of the respondents also mentioned Inquiry as an important issue of the *pathos* of an authentic Christian postmodern leader.

These postmodern leaders each asserted that postmoderns perceive the authenticity, authority, and integrity of a preacher through his or her ability to ask questions. The postmodern person is especially uninterested in preachers who arrive with their pre-packaged answers. The postmodern person wants to meet preachers who are on the journey of communal discovery with them. These emergent leaders suggest that effective postmodern preachers will use questions as an important tool to help their congregations grow spiritually.

R5 described his church as "open-ended." He said, "We would rather leave people with a good question than a glib answer. We do not have a conclusion to a lot of our studies." Similarly, R8 said, "There is a lot of freedom to work the crowd a little differently.... In the middle of that preaching/teaching time we have had them turn to each other and deal with a question." R4 said,

> As we really thoroughly look at some of the questions that they are asking and some of the struggles that they are dealing with, when we take those questions and we push them as far as they can go, we can then push them even a little bit further. That is effective but difficult preaching. As you are delivering [a sermon] and as you are throwing out a question, when the congregation looks at the preacher after asking that question and says, "I cannot believe you found that question. I have been dealing with that question and struggling with that question. I have been afraid to ask that question for a very, very long time. There you are in front of this community and you are asking that difficult question." There is a point of identification with the community that I think is very healthy in grappling and discovering God's word.

Postmoderns perceive this allowing of inquiry and uncertainty, even into the very act of preaching, as authentic Christian *pathos* in a preacher. R1 believes in leading his people on a journey of inquiry. He said, "For example, if you're going to do something about politics, well, why not bring up the politicians and ask?" R2 said he publicly approaches preaching with a series of questions: "Am I interpreting this correctly? Am I translating this correctly? Are we taking it from what it meant to those people and putting it into what it is to us? Is that true to what the Bible says?" In the same way, R9 said he teaches his people to ask, "What did it mean for the people it was first written for?"

R4 said, "I think [this affinity with inquiry] has to do with the subjectivity of the postmodern era." He said he believes that postmoderns are "not coming from that vantage point where there is an objective standard of truth.... It is just not part of the fabric of what people believe today." This affects his approach to preaching. R6 has invited his community into the exegetical process by posting his questions about the Bible texts on the Internet. R3 said he does the same thing, asking his congregation about the texts, "What would you emphasize? What questions would you bring to it? What proclamations would you derive from it?" R7 said, "By asking questions there is participating and interacting and furnishing people's imaginations." R4 pointed out that Jesus' method of communication was predominantly to tell stories and ask questions, while modern Christianity writes a lot of essays that get preached and gives answers. He said, "I think we have to look at the methodology of Scripture as maybe an approach." R10 also complained about the too-ready answer in preaching. She said, "I'll raise the questions that that topic raises.... I want to be informed enough about the topic to make helpful contributions to the discussion and ask appropriate questions.... I have to do more research and be more prepared for other people's questions." R4 said, "It seems like God repents and changes his mind with Moses. We are told at times that God does not change his mind. I have to live with some sort of sacred ambiguity at certain times."

Each of the emergent church subjects communicated the primary issue of Inquiry as a vital part of the authentic *pathos* of the postmodern preacher. They each suggested that the successful emergent biblical expositor must have the obvious *pathos* of an inquiring fellow journeyer on the path of the Christian spiritual life to have the kind of integrity that wins a hearing for the *logos* in this postmodern *ethos*.

C. Irreverence

Each of the respondents also identified and demonstrated aspects of the primary issue of Irreverence as a vital part of the authentic *pathos* of the emergent preacher. They all demonstrated reverence for some aspects of historical Christianity. But they also all displayed irreverence for what they perceived as modernist impositions on authentic Christian faith. R4 commented, "Many emerging church leaders are looking at the chaos that they are surrounded in and the death of Christendom. Church is not a playground anymore to play around in." He said, "We are not in Jerusalem anymore. There is this notion that we are in Babylon. We are a church in exile. We have to be more missional."

R1 does not come from a Christian background. He said, "I'm not that soaked in church culture, but I'm not entirely happy in it or necessarily willing to play by all of its rules." He is the one who sometimes holds services in a nightclub or pub and does communion with meat pies and beer. R10 described what she sees as the main problem of the traditional, modernist, institutional Church, saying, "The problem with the institutional church is the need to preserve the institution." She said she has the "challenge" of trying to fit her ministry into a modernist, institutional church structure.

One can also see how this casual *pathos* is displayed in the loose and irreverent language of the respondents. R7 said, "What we need to do is get rid of crap preaching." Later, he reacted to the "seeker-sensitive" movement in America, saying, "Expository preaching was dry and arrogant. It does not do anything." He said that people like "Rick Warren and Bill Hybels and all these other people [with] their kind of preaching ... have just sold out." He said they are "a bunch of pricks." He speaks like this not to shock, but because this is the raw authentic *pathos* with which he is comfortable and is understood by his contemporaries. This is part of the *pathos* integrity for his *ethos*. Likewise, R4 said about the previous generation's leadership, "It is a damn good thing they have had good theology and been brought up in that kind of heritage because had they not been informed by that good theology, their preaching could go anywhere."

These emergent leaders not only casually use words that some in a previous generation may find offensive, they also casually challenge long-held sacred ideas about church. R9 said, "I am quite pro short sermons." He said he thinks it makes it "harder to communicate having only half the time." He also said he doesn't like preaching that "comes down to the black and white conversion experience. 'You're out and you are in.' I do not think [the Gospel] is quite like that."

Many of the respondents made irreverent comments towards what was perceived to be obsolete forms of the modernist church. R2 recognized the "trap of sometimes using [outdated words and religious concepts] like 'repent' or 'blessing.'" He wants to use new words to give these words their original meanings. R3 stated his disdain for spoiled words like "evangelical," saying, "Evangelical is such a slippery word. It seems like all the vocabulary is getting a little slippery."

R7 even challenged the metaphor of "substitutionary atonement" as a revered concept: "It is based on penal substitution," which he said he believes does not relate to our postmodern context. He complained, "[The term] 'biblical preaching' is a euphemism for giving the Gospel in a propositional, four-point, four spiritual laws [format]." He called preaching that only says "pray this prayer and when you die" a "sales pitch." Instead, he said he uses "the word 'Christus Victor'[203] as a concept for explaining Christ's death and resurrection," and he is "certainly finding that the postmodern people, the new Christians, can engage with that."

R7 talked about a friend of his who described the modernist Gospel message as "You suck! In fact, you suck so badly God was

---

203   "Christus Victor" (Christ the Victor) is the title of Gustaf Aulen's 1931 classic work on the atonement. He explored the Early Church's stress on the ransom metaphor to explain Jesus' victory over the evil powers of sin, death, and the devil, which hold humanity in bondage.

so cross that he killed his son." He said, "That is the message that [postmodern] people are not responsive to at all." He said that some [modernist] Christians would argue, saying, "Well, that is the message. You need to thank God that he killed his son to spare you." Rather, wanting to communicate with a *pathos* that his audience will listen to, he wants to use "other metaphors for the atonement … maybe one that may be easier for people to engage with." R7 even irreverently said, "If getting rid of Sunday services [or] preaching for awhile [can solve the problem of people experiencing reductionist bad preaching] then great!" Challenging what may be concepts revered by a previous generation, he said,

> I think when biblical preaching gets reduced to Gospel preaching in that "reductionist" kind of way, effectively what you have is something for people to do so they get to heaven when they die.… What happens is the Gospel is primarily dealing with one thing: how do you stop feeling guilty and get to heaven when you die? What that does not do is give much space at all for doing anything in this life. The old adage when I became a Christian was Jesus is your Lord and Savior. He has to do both. I think what happens for a lot of Christians is, "well, I am tired. I am exhausted. I have limited resources. I will go to heaven when I die. I might feel pretty guilty about not doing Christian things now." I think biblical preaching would furnish people and say, "Christianity is not about going to heaven when you die. That is not the mission. That is not what he proclaimed." Jesus proclaimed an alternative way of living, one of the consequences of which is we start it in this life and it continues for eternity.

R4 also disparaged the approach to preaching that evokes a modernist kind of authority, saying, "There is not that grid in which someone can simply say, 'because the Bible says' or 'thus sayeth the

Lord.' We are probably talking two generations ago when that was happening." There is a casualness to the approach to church these emergent leaders described. This is a disregard for those things, which are deemed unimportant, though a past generation may have reverenced them.

R8 described his 11:20 AM emergent generation-oriented church service, saying, "It's the last one of the morning. Everybody … has slept in … and it's dressed down a little bit just in terms of the feel. It is guitar and band driven.… There is a lot of freedom to work the crowd a little differently." R9 stated that at his church, "The sermon is usually no more than twenty minutes long. The one thing I have seen a lot in the past in what I will call normal Baptist churches, ones that would not claim to be emerging at all, [is that] they would have sermons that would be forty-five minutes or an hour long. Those are things that we have abandoned in some respects." Likewise, R6 complained about modernist approaches to "biblical preaching," saying, "What I do not like about the phrase 'biblical preaching' is that it presumes that as long as we talk about the text, that is enough. We have been biblical."

R10 explained how her worship service incorporates "secular music," "secular videos," and "prayers and readings that come from other faith traditions." These things contrast what was commonly revered in modernist services of a past generation. Some might find R5's worship space and program somewhat irreverent. He described,

> Our worship environment is a lounge with round tables. Usually a family would have a table to themselves. There is a coffee machine there and people can get up and get drinks at any stage. We often center in on activities at the table. Sometimes we have stations and we may have a journey that people take through different activities. Sometimes we preach. Sometimes not.

All ten of these emergent church leaders described the importance of the primary issue of Irreverence in the practice of exposing their congregations to the Word of God. The emergent biblical expositor must have the discernable *pathos* of irreverence for those things (religious and secular) that may not be essential to the Gospel, but may be merely revered by a past generation, to have the kind of perceived authenticity, authority, and integrity that wins a hearing for the *logos* in this postmodern *ethos*.

The Logos of Postmodern Preaching

A. Relevancy

The authentic *logos* of Christian preaching is the message content of the texts of God's Word. Each of the respondents articulated aspects of the primary issue of Relevancy as a vital part of the *logos* of meaningful postmodern preaching. R5 explained his vision for wanting "to have a style of church that will be relevant to life as the early [thirty-somethings] experience it, [and] that relates through to people of other ages." When asked how he would define "biblical preaching," R5 said it is simply "hitting the main themes of the passage that relate to how we live." He elaborated, "We then see which ones are relevant to our lives today.... Those points that are relevant become the preaching points.... It was preaching in a way that is relevant to people." Later, he commented that he does not believe preaching to be "relevant," saying,

> I do not believe preaching is relevant to the emerging church really.... When we went and opened the new congregation intentionally with the emerging group without preaching sections, it just seemed to be the preaching was not relevant. There was a hunger for God's Word, a hunger for a sense of going on a journey, but not a desire to be preached at.

His point is that when church attendees perceive themselves as "preached at," it is no longer "relevant." A "hunger for God's Word" remains relevant. When asked how he would define "biblical preaching," R9 said that it was "being true to the text [or Bible] and ensuring application that fits into the context of the people sitting listening at the time of the sermon." He outlined the important steps to doing this, saying, "When you can figure out [the original] meaning, I think then you can take that, and through the context that I am preaching into, quite often it is truth that is timeless." He said he tries to "figure out those truths that are timeless and apply them into a context now. I guess I am trying to see how it is going to relate to the people that I am going to be talking to." R1 simply said, "I'm often looking for connection."

For some, there is a stigma around the word "relevant." R6 said, "The authority of God is written in the text and [a preacher makes] that text relevant to a group of people." Then he stumbled on the word "relevant," saying, "By relevant I do not mean, what do I mean by relevant?" He recovered and said, "By relevant I mean that they are aware of the fact that God speaks and is alive and active and wants to challenge and grow them today. I do not mean relevant as in McDonald's." The word "relevant" can be trendy or shallow or compromised. R2 said, "I have a lot of friends doing 'What Homer Simpson would say to whomever.'" He confessed that he wonders about the validity of "that take on it." But, he said, "I have friends working with people who are theologically ignorant and they preach the Word. Congregations love it as well. It is the Word of God." His point seems to be that if one can get "theologically ignorant" people to listen to the Bible by presenting it through topics like "What Homer Simpson would say to whomever," then "it is the Word of God."

R7 questioned what actually makes a church "relevant." He talked about the fallacy of merely abandoning supposed modernist traditions to gain "relevancy." He said, "What [some people] think is that if you get rid of all of those [modernist] things they will not [be modern]. Therefore, this will be incredibly liberating and we will have this extremely relevant church community that everybody will want to connect to." He pointed out, "In practice, that is not the case. I have not seen it." He said that this was especially true of preaching:

> One of the dangers is that too many people think we need to get rid of preaching. [They say,] "It is completely irrelevant...." I am bit tired of people saying, "Preaching is dead because you stand up and you speak and everyone is forced to listen. It is completely irrelevant." What do people do all day when they are watching television? They do not say anything. They just sit there. [But] there is storytelling going on. There is imagination is going on. They are asking questions. They are thinking about things.... The idea that preaching is irrelevant, I think, is nonsense.

R3 said he preaches to "awaken the faith of people [and] proclaim the Gospel. He wants to "use the Gospel to critique the culture [and] proclaim the reign of God in a world that is too comfortable with status quo." He believes that the *logos* of Christian proclamation is relevant, but he also suggested that it must be contextualized in his contemporary *ethos* to be received. He must understand what is relevant to the receptor audience to be able to contextualize it. This is what R4 meant when he said, "I think as we exegete our communities ... there is a point of identification with the community.... I think before we have any authority and before we can inspire we have to identify with our community."

When asked what the most important task of a leader is, R8 answered, "I think allowing people to use their own story in the emergent church to intersect with the Gospel of Jesus Christ is where the preaching is going to happen.... I have always been in that culture of youth and their families. If I'm not connecting with them, I'm not connecting." When asked the same question, R10 answered, "Rather than just putting up signs saying, 'come here,' we are going about moving out into the world where people are." She explained how she uses all the relevant media available within the *ethos* of her congregation to explore the *logos* of the Word: "I think that we need to be creative enough to have different styles in different settings, and I think that there's a place for, you know, divergent styles."

R1 concluded, asking, "As Christians, how do we stand? Do we stand apart from culture or are we in the midst of culture?" He continued, "I'm wanting the stories [the *logos*] to come life.… It's no good if it's dry and listless and 'out there.' It has to link with here." R6 said, "I am the servant of the community, and therefore, the text needs to speak to the issues, the questions, the encouragement that the community has around this text. If nothing happened, and sometimes it did not, sometimes the text would not engage at all. There was still the sense that I was forcing my community to be more biblical because they at least had to read it."

All ten of these emergent church leaders described the importance of the primary issue of Relevancy in the practice of exposing their congregations to the Word of God. As has been true of every preacher in every era, the emergent biblical expositor must connect the *logos* of God's Word to the relevant, real-life *ethos* of his contemporary audience.

B. Necessity

All of the subjects also confessed the necessity of preaching the *logos* of God's Word to their contemporary *ethos*. R4 simply said, "I think expository preaching is necessary for the emerging generation." R8 stated, "The whole idea of story and the biblical story is so important." R9 said, "The church that I am part of would claim to be emerging. It still has a sermon slot every week. By having that the statement is that preaching is still significant.… You still have to communicate the truth."

When asked if expository preaching is relevant to the emerging church, R2 said, "Oh yeah!" He said, "I think that if you take the Word of God and explain what it is saying, people of all generations and all different places can understand and relate.… I do not see another way, I guess, than telling what the Word of God is saying." Asked the same question, R1 responded, "My experience has been that actually the people I'm dealing with want to know that we are wrestling with the Bible." When asked the same question, R7 said, "Hugely! We have found it to be the biggest evangelistic tool that we have had.... There is definitely a place for preaching. We need it.... Absolutely! Definitely!" Likewise, R5 said, "Yes! I am into exposing God's Word. We are really enthusiastic about it.... There [is] a hunger for God's Word!"

When asked to identify the most important task of a leader in the emerging church, R2 responded by saying, "Leading people to the Word of God." Similarly, R3 said he sees it as his job to "teach the Bible in a culture that is largely biblically illiterate." R10 said, "Certainly the Bible is the core source of the information that we're communicating.... The Bible is the means through which the truth is explained." Likewise, R6 said, "My job is to grow a healthy, vibrant, empowering community.... Preaching would be an important part of that.... To me the Bible is so important that it has to be accessed in a whole lot of ways."

All ten of these emergent church leaders described the importance of the primary issue of the Necessity of the practice of preaching the authentic *logos* content of the revealed texts of God's Word to their congregations. These postmodern leaders suggested that the emergent postmodern Christian leader must be confident that this task is vital and be confident in doing it.

C. Text

Finally, each of the respondents also articulated aspects of the primary issue of Text as a vital part of the authentic *logos* of meaningful emergent preaching. Though each of these emergent church leaders was fully steeped in the postmodern culture, preached primarily to a young, postmodern *ethos*, and gave serious attention to embodying an authentically postmodern *pathos*, they each were fully committed to understanding and proclaiming the text of the Scriptures as the authoritative Word of God. R2 shared,

> I guess I have just been impressed with the effectiveness of God's Word as the message that is taught passage by passage.... [I] was affected and changed and impressed by God's Word being expressed by different people, the same book but a different perspective coming out.... I think I grew up thinking that preaching had a lot to do with fun stories. My sense now is I try to entertain only so that I can accurately ... portray the message of the text.

When R1 said that "the people [he was] dealing with want to know that we are wrestling with the Bible," he specifically mentioned the Bible. It is this text that is the *logos* of Christian proclamation. When R3 said he wanted to "teach the Bible in a culture that is largely biblically illiterate," he was talking about exegeting and proclaiming the meaning of specific texts. He said Christian proclamation is "proclaiming the cross and not just the feel-good values that come out of the Bible, but proclaiming Christ crucified and risen." R6 agreed, saying, "One of the things we did at [our church] was we worked very hard at what it meant to empower the community to have a sense of engagement with that biblical text. That might be through telling a story in relation to the text, inputting into the shape of the sermon, or reflecting beforehand on the Bible text."

R8 said he includes attention to the Bible as one of the "non-negotiables" of authentic Christian discipleship. He said, "The marks of discipleship are six non-negotiable disciple-making disciplines ... daily prayer, weekly worship, daily reading of the Bible, serving, relating to others for spiritual growth, and giving." R6 is committed to helping his congregation engage with the Bible text. He said, "We need biblical reflection in our culture, in our world. Anything I could do to help my community engage more with the Bible was a good thing."

R5 described helping his congregation engage the texts of the book of Daniel: "We are just trying to take each passage as it comes. I am looking at this now and asking, 'What are the main things of Daniel 12?'" R1 was also engaging the texts of the book of Daniel at the time of this study. He explained how he engaged his audience with the biblical texts:

> Looking at Daniel chapter one: It's the start of the school year for us and Daniel is off to school. So Daniel is a student.... So, you name [stories about starting school from his audience] and they're telling their stories. And the next thing you do is you tell one of God's stories. So then you come into the book of Daniel itself and tell a bit about the background and that is the point when you're kind of getting the two stories intermingled, and I think that's where it actually happens.... So again, we're trying to connect to the story there and our stories now.

These emergent church leaders want to get the message of the *logos* right. R8 said, "I always teach people when we're dealing with the Bible that you have to know what it meant then before you can deal with what it would mean now." He also said, "It becomes important for the preacher to know the historical context of what was going on before he or she can deal with the present context of what is going on now.... otherwise we miss too much stuff." R2 said, "I have found a tremendous amount of strength and encouragement when I go to the text and try to read it devotionally first and then really dig deep and find out what the message of the passage is. What was Christ saying? What was Paul trying to get across to the people and then how does that apply to us?"

R7 almost apologetically described his church's commitment to the biblical texts, admitting, "We are going to spend six months working through the book of Romans." He pointed to the common perception that emergent churches do not have regular Bible exposition. He said, "I am not saying you cannot do it, but if that is what most people are doing, there is definitely a place for it." He declared his commitment to do expositional teaching of Bible texts:

> We have gone through the book of James. We called the title of that "How to Live Well." It was great for us to spend a period of time, I think we spent twelve weeks, and we went through that very deeply. It still had a lot to do with application and participation. We spent a lot of time reading Gospel stories. We worked our way completely through the book of Mark. In autumn, we are planning to spend the whole of Sunday morning having the Gospel of Mark read to us out loud from start to finish. We will then work our way through it.

Many of the respondents complained about what they perceived as false ideas of what "expository preaching" has come to represent. R10, who said, "Certainly the Bible is the core source of the information that we're communicating," shared that she lives in a "conservative community" where people will ask, "Have you preached the Bible?" or "Do you preach the Bible?" But she said she believes if you "flesh that out," what the people mean, it is things like, "Do you teach women to be subservient to men?" She complained about what she called "fundamentalist, conservative approaches to text." Similarly, R1 complained, "What I've found difficult is that when you talk about 'expository preaching,' what pops into mind is the one person who says, 'And now we're going to go through the next five verses of John, chapter eight. We're going to rip all its guts out and lay it on the table.'" He said, "I'm not sure that there is a huge future for that in its own right."

R5 said he had "grown up with a style of preaching that really wants to go through verse by verse and state everything that the passage says and what it means within the context which it was written in." He said, "It really makes the point of preaching [to be] passing on knowledge about the Bible." Then he said, "My approach is more to look at the passage and try to see what the main things it is saying is rather than all the little details." R7 said, "One of the problems with 'biblical preaching' is [it is] reductionist to preaching the four spiritual laws. There is nothing to teach. You can maybe make that last as many different ways as possible for a couple of years. Then you are done. There is nothing for anybody else to learn." But he said, "By telling the Bible stories, it is completely inexhaustive. With the Bible stories you can even go back to them a year later and say, 'Do we see these differently now at the church?'"

R1 also offered a different vision for authentic "expository preaching" by describing a symbol for it:

> If you think of the Bible as being a river, there's lots of currents in a river—the main current, but there's also back eddies and kind of side currents and every so often another stream will join. So, I would hope that expository preaching would be a part of swimming in that river. And where expository preaching has dropped the ball and has been quite damaging has been when it is focusing on a tiny bit of the river and missing the big current, the location of that bit.

Similarly, R7 used a symbol to describe what he believed authentic "expository preaching" ought to be. He said, "Real 'biblical preaching' would be storytelling just as our family history." He explained, "These are our family poetry books. These are our family photo albums: snapshots, blogs, journals, you name it. These are the things that collectively give us a window into retelling how God has interacted with his people over time." Relating that to Bible teaching, he said, "We have church history. We need to tell our story. We need to locate ourselves in that story. I think 'biblical preaching' would do that—furnish our imaginations and retell the story."

All of these respondents exposed their commitment to the texts of the Bible. R6 explained, "There is still a huge amount of place to respect Scripture because it is an ancient text; therefore, it is deeply spiritual and a guide for people." He said, "This text is primary in our lives." Similarly, R4 revealed his great love for and commitment to the biblical texts:

> I have an incredible love for Scripture that was passed on to me in a conservative, evangelical environment. That is the heritage in which I come out of. We were taught to believe that these words were God's words from a very, very early age. It was these stories that I was told and some of these Psalms ... that I was read to as a child. These stories were intoxicating to my imagination and given special position in my imagination.... [But, people at my church] are not familiar with the text. They are approaching the Scripture thinking, "What is going on?" When they are reading a book that is up to six thousand years old ... I have a sensitivity towards these people.... They desire to read this text personally and understand it personally.... That informs the way that I communicate. It certainly informs my desire to communicate the whole of Scripture and to deal with difficult texts and to communicate how we can read these texts. God has inspired these texts regardless of their difficulty.... [At our church] we do not avoid difficult texts. We do not pretend to do topical sermons or pretend to do full books and lay over really what is more of a topical approach. We really go from beginning to end.

Each of the ten respondents talked about how the Bible is a central part of their emergent church services. Some of them may not "preach" in a traditional sense, but they are all committed to attending to the *logos* of the Scriptures and communicating its message. In the following excerpts from the interviews, each of the respondents described their habits for exegeting the biblical texts of the Scriptures to help them understand the *logos* for preaching to their congregations:

R1:

> I have a series of commentaries and pour over them as much as I can. I run a copy of *Bibleworks* with some of the great exegesis stuff, which I'm not brilliant at. I read anything I can and if you have the timeframe, then, to bounce things off people is incredibly helpful.

R2:

> I try and do [exegesis] myself first and then I compare what I have come up with to see what people have come [up with] before me.... I will go through it and have Greek with me.... I use a lot of commentaries.... I will buy three or four books.... I usually have two or three commentary-ish books or theological books.

R3:

> Taking the text from its biblical context. The Gospel for this coming Sunday is the parable of "The Prodigal Son." That text is out of Luke. He is the only Gospel writer who proclaims or tries to understand what Jesus was trying to communicate with that parable. How Jesus is portrayed [and how he] dialogued with the Pharisees in that chapter ... once situating it in its historical, biblical context, first century Palestine, and then trying to understand it in a twenty-first century North American context.

R4:

> There is a whole process that is involved in study. I have a rudimentary understanding of languages. As best as I can, I will proceed with not just

commentaries but scholarship to try to get at the root of the text. For those particular texts that I have trouble understanding the Greek, I will consult various translations. I will consult scholars that understand Greek. That is the beautiful thing about technology and communication today. I have friends who are various scholars in various institutions that I can consult and say, "I do not understand this text. Can you help me understand the Greek or the Hebrew surrounding this?" When I say study that is what I mean—studying commentaries.

R5:

I have never studied Hebrew so I do not have much of an understanding of the Hebrew. I have studied Greek and really know enough Greek to be able to read a commentary on the Greek text. I do that sort of thing.

R6:

Often I will use Bible commentaries just to gain some perspective, an interpretation commentary series, for example. I will try to choose a range.... I find that very helpful in order to determine the main issue. I will then use a number of translations. In my early days, I used to try and translate it from the Greek myself. I do not have that time. I will often drop a bit of Greek or a bit of Hebrew.

R7:

We did the book of Philippians two and a half years ago. I spent a great deal of time researching that and reading through it. It is my preferred learning style. I did not sit down and say, "Right, we are doing this passage this week. I am going to spend all of Friday preparing." I would do a lot of research up front and then I would do less week-by-week. That has now changed.… I spend a great deal of time studying the Bible, doing theology.… For me, instead of, "I have to think of a topic and I have to go away for a day to prepare it," preaching has become, "How do I take what I have been learning and living in my church community and all of those experiences and all that learning and apply that through a teaching time on a Sunday?"

R8:

I will just read [it] devotionally on Monday morning. I'll go to Starbucks and sit down.… I might read it a couple times and I'll just ask myself, "What is going on here? What is the context…? Now I won't maybe write anything down but just kind of look at it devotionally. On Tuesday, I'll keep thinking about that and I may ask a few questions of my colleagues here about "The last time you read that, was there anything that sticks out? If you have looked at the text as a horizon, is there anything that pops up?" Then I'll just kind of let that filter. So I'll go to a hockey game and I'll pay attention to [it].… I'll go to a concert and I'll pay attention to [it].… You know, this text finds its way into my, sort of, my daily life.… Along about a week later, on the next Monday, the day before I have to present my thinking to my colleagues, I'll sit down and try to funnel it down to like three or four major points. And I really try to find a different twist in a familiar story.… I'll get those three or four major points and I'll then let them sort of stew a little bit. I might go to *Homiletics Online* then and I'll look for somebody's story that's sort of engaging around that whole idea. And then the next day, Tuesday, I have the hour before I'm going to present it blocked off for me to get real specific about the kind of direction that I'm going.... I'll have read commentaries the day before and the days before and then on that Tuesday. Then, in the hour before I pull that all together, I hit the printer and take that to the table with my colleagues.... I have some Interpreter Bible Commentary things that I have not used in recent years. There are times when I can go back to [Greek and Hebrew] and once in a while I'll go back and I'll dig out a word.

R9:

I read it in the NRSV. I like using something a little bit more conversational like the Message. Then I would also use the NIV just as another comparison. If there are things that are not clear or I would to have another spin on it. I like to get it in my head and then sit on it for a little bit.... To find the context of the Bible stuff, I print it out on an 8" by 4" with a thin column down the page. I might recall different words that are repeated or things that I think are significant. I might get a list of different people who are speaking in this passage of Scripture.... I might write their names at the top of the page and then I would write down what his point of view in the story is, who is telling the story, and what the genre of the text might be. The outcome of the story and the perspective of who is telling the story.... With a repeated word, something like "light," it might be repeated three or four times. I will look into that. Some translations might use different words than "light...." I do a bit of background study. I guess I sit on it for a while.... I would start my preparation on a Tuesday.... When I would pick it up again, I would not have been thinking about it continually over those few days, I might see something differently. I guess I am trying to see how it is going to relate to the people that I am going to be talking to. I want them to know the summary of what I have found out from my looking at the text and what it means. I want them to be able to understand it. I might be able to tell them black and white this is what the text is trying to say. But that's not always easy for them to take away. I might sort of find different ways of packaging that. Saying the same thing but saying it in ways that people can relate it to their own lives or their own context I guess. Context is very important to me.... One thing that I do right at the end of my little research is look at the commentary.... I have not studied Greek or Hebrew. I get a bit bogged down if I am reading a commentary that is just full of lots of information about the Greek text. I generally avoid that stuff.... If I am looking at a text I will often look through an interlinear Bible. I cannot speak Greek and I could not read it on its own, but with an interlinear Bible with the English above it, I have basic skills. I am not ignorant to the Greek.

R10:

I have a couple of different commentaries that I use. I use sometimes, not every week by any stretch of the imagination, but I do pull out my Greek New Testament. I do pull out my Greek sometimes.

These statements demonstrate several things about the respondents' attitudes toward and practice of the exegetical process. First, most of the subjects demonstrated a commitment to at least try and engage the texts in their original languages (R2, R4, R5, R8, R9, and R10), though a few confessed their lack of language skills, and one (R6) said he did not have time for this any more. Some said they regularly consulted colleagues (R1, R4, and R8). Most of them specifically mentioned using commentaries (R1, R2, R4, R5, R6, R8, R9, and R10). Two subjects mentioned specific electronic resource aids: *Bibleworks* (R1) and *Homiletics Online* (R8).

All ten of these emergent church leaders described the importance of the primary issue of Text in the practice of exposing their congregations to the *logos* of the Word of God. Though they have a range of abilities and habits in exegeting the biblical texts, they all share a commitment to engaging the Bible as the source for the *logos* of their messages. They share a commitment to keeping attention on the Bible as a central part of their church services. In summary, the nine primary issues—Community, Activity, Sensuality, Humility, Inquiry, Irreverence, Relevancy, Necessity, and Text—provide a glimpse into the sermonic process among these ten postmodern preachers.

The data demonstrates how these emerging church leaders understand the postmodern context and its influence on their ministry and preaching. It reveals how these emerging church leaders attempt to contextualize their sermons and how this contextualization is especially reflected within the praxis of their preaching. It also shows how biblical truth is incorporated into the meetings of their postmodern congregations, and how the actual practices of preaching reflect the practical, theological, and philosophical perspectives of these representative leaders.

The Findings

This project explored the attitudes of ten postmodern church leaders towards preaching and their practice of the sermonic process within the context of the Spiritual formation of their emergent congregations. The goal was to provide research to study this primary inquiry and to discover in what ways it is both authentically Christian and authentically postmodern.

Because the nature of most of the representative congregations in this study was of a younger age and made up of many new believers, the *pathos* of the conveyors becomes even more vital. A mature believer should be able to see past the perceived integrity of the conveyor of the message to the eternal meaning of the message. A less mature believer will be more easily distracted by an insensitive conveyor with little perceived integrity.

The scope of this research project was to determine an answer to the question, What is the attitude towards and practice of the function of preaching within the context of the Spiritual formation of their postmodern congregations? The conclusion of this chapter is a synthesis and evaluation of the findings of the exploration, with recommendations for further study and suggestions for future practice of Christian Spiritual formation through preaching in the postmodern context. Five secondary questions guided me in an inductive analysis of the data collected.

The first secondary research question was, How do some emerging church leaders understand the postmodern context and its influence on ministry and preaching? The research data demonstrated that each of the ten research respondents had a clear grasp of their postmodern context. They all demonstrated a concern for their generational and regional contexts and a desire to see their contemporaries understand and participate in an authentic experience of the Church of Jesus Christ. Each respondent was committed to providing a church environment that was authentically postmodern and authentically Christian. Through their own analysis of biblical Christianity and their contemporary culture, these emergent Christian leaders were experimenting with many new forms of public proclamation, endeavoring to understand, along with their congregations, what the Christian faith ought to look like in their setting.

The second secondary question was, How do emerging church leaders attempt to contextualize their sermons? The research data confirmed that all ten respondents worked hard at contextualizing their preaching to their contemporary audience. Each of the respondents demonstrated sensitivity to their postmodern contexts by incorporating an attention to collective involvement in their interpretation and proclamation of the Scriptures. They also gave attention to dynamic involvement in application for their action-oriented congregations. They had explored full five-sense engagements within their church service experience. They all articulated commitments to leading their congregations through journeys of investigation, rather than religious programs of ready answers. They also all demonstrated a modesty and self-deprecating humor in their manner and approach to leadership. There was a general irreverence toward many of the things that modernist church leaders may reverence, such as formal language and dress, while revering those things that their postmodern context reveres but may be ignored by most modernist church leaders, such as the environment, global justice, and poverty.

The third secondary question was, How is this contextualization reflected within their praxis of preaching? The research data showed that all ten of the respondents have a commitment to regular teaching of biblical principles, if not true expository preaching. This demonstrates that all ten of the respondents believe that preaching is necessary for their emergent congregations, but only if done in a relevant way. To ensure that their messages are relevant, each of the respondents described ways in which they engage their contemporaries in the very basic levels of exegesis of their preaching texts. They invite their contemporaries into the essential questions of the text and invite their congregations to establish the very topics that they will address in their sermons.

They also spent time in their cultural environments, exploring popular media, meanings, and methods, and looking for cultural tools and themes to bridge the biblical message and their audience. They demonstrated a deep understanding of their contemporary cultures and a deep concern for biblical truth. All of the respondents were steeped in their contemporary culture. While another generation of Christian leaders may have had a more negative view of popular culture, these postmodern leaders embraced their contemporary culture and utilized its music, movies, and heroes to connect their sermons to their audience. It was evident in the interviews that this was not just a method these leaders used to communicate, but rather, each respondent demonstrated a positive participation in and enjoyment of his or her popular contemporary culture.

The fourth secondary question was, How is biblical truth incorporated into the meeting of a postmodern congregation? The research data indicated that all of the respondents incorporated the Bible into their church services in some way. This did not always involve a traditional sermon. The Scriptures were usually read, sung, prayed, or discussed by each of the representative emergent congregations. Sometimes biblical themes were merely suggested during group discussions. This was the data that created the evidence for greatest concern. The careful handling of the biblical texts varied between the respondents and also varied between the weeks of a given respondent's church service. Though a common theme of respect for the Scriptures was evident, the careful attention to exegesis and exposition was inconsistent. One concern is that while emphasizing the need to change the style of public church proclamation to make it more palatable to a postmodern audience, these emergent church leaders may be compromising the vital practice of exposing God's people to the actual messages of God's Word. There is a need to avoid the "brokenness"[204] of the modernist approach to preaching for the postmodern audience, while establishing an unbroken way of exposing postmodern believers to the Word of God. These emerging church leaders are responding to the challenge of engaging a contemporary culture, which disdains what "preaching" has come to be perceived as. Yet it is concerning that a clear, essential purpose for preaching was not articulated by these respondents for their greater understanding and commitment.

An essential task of the Church in each generation and region is to guard the true nature of the Church from any compromises with its contemporary context. The Church is God's covenant community in every time and culture, confirming and engaging God's presence and truth, while correcting and rebuking the inherent untruths in every time and culture. Rather than "reinventing the Church,"[205] the Church must authentically be the Church for this next generation. Each new generation must throw off the cultural baggage of the last

---

204   Pagitt, Faithworks Magazine, July 2004.
205   McLaren, The Church on the Other Side: Doing Ministry in the Postmodern Matrix.

generation to reform authentic Christian faith in its new context. But there is always the danger of picking up what could be worse baggage from this contemporary culture. Modernism was primarily a reaction to premodernism; postmodernism is a reaction to modernism. It must be admitted that in every way postmodernism judges modernism as wrong, it is right. Unfortunately, though, postmodernism sets up a just-as-wrong alternative to biblical revelation.

The final secondary question was, How do the actual practices of preaching reflect practical, theological, and philosophical perspectives? The data verified that there is evidence of inconsistency among emergent church leaders in the area of biblical exposition, and a need for greater understanding of the essential purpose and practice of preaching in postmodern, Western churches. All of the research respondents demonstrated a concern that their churches be "missional."[206] But if their churches are primarily outreach vehicles for unchurched or post-churched postmoderns, where will committed, believing postmodern Christians be raised towards greater Christian maturity? If these emergent churches are trying to reach out to their postmodern contemporaries through "dumbing down"[207] the message and practice of being Church, where and how will the lifelong theological and moral formation of God's people happen?

This has traditionally happened through the regular exposition of the Scriptures through preaching. Attention to the regular exposition of God's Word must be retained and strengthened in emergent churches. Emergent church leaders must understand their vital role as exposers of God's Word. They must be trained in and held responsible for the careful exegesis of the *logos* of God's Holy Scriptures and the continued sensitivity to their contemporary *ethos*, while developing their authentic *pathos* integrity.

While it may be argued that the Apostles did preach topical messages in Acts, it can be understood that these messages were for itinerant evangelism. Meanwhile, the Church retained the regular

206   Guder and Barrett, Missional Church: A Vision for the Sending of the Church in North America.
207   Marv J. Dawn, Reaching Out Without Dumbing Down: A Theology of Worship for the Turn-of-the-Century Culture.

practice of weekly devotion to scriptural exposition for Spiritual formation. The texts of this exposition were initially only the Old Testament. Later, when the Apostles and their associates wrote their epistles to the churches, these texts were received as Scripture and were read and taught in the churches with authority equal to the Old Testament. For theological and moral formation, the Christian Church followed the practices of Moses in the desert, the Levites in the Temple, Ezra in the remnant, the Rabbis in the synagogues, and Jesus in his incarnation of developing Spiritual maturity through leading their contemporary audience in the systematic exegesis and exposition of the texts of the Holy Scriptures.

Like many of the leaders and authors within the emergent church scene, the research respondents demonstrated a deep concern for the evangelization (or re-evangelization) of their contemporaries. This is laudable and essential. It is the will of God and the goal of the Church of Jesus Christ. Yet there remains a need for churches to nurture the committed postmodern Christian person to maturity. If Western emergent churches are primarily evangelistic endeavors, there may be little maturity in theological or moral formation among postmodern Christians.

The data demonstrated that these emergent church leaders were rejecting the "bathwater" of modernist Christianity, while attempting to retain the "baby" of the essential Christian faith. In this endeavor, they were pioneering new ways of giving attention to the revealed Word of God in public worship. They may have reacted to terms associated with modernism like "expository preaching," or even "biblical preaching," yet they remained committed to exposing their congregations to the messages of the Bible.

The nine important themes that surfaced from the data analysis reflect a shift from a modernist approach to Spiritual formation through preaching towards an authentically postmodern and Christian approach. The nine primary issues—Community, Activity, Sensuality, Humility, Inquiry, Irreverence, Relevancy, Necessity, and Text—provide a glimpse of what is happening in the state of the current practice of Christian preaching in postmodern congregations. These nine issues can be explored to provide a grid for observing the state of current practice, and to give us direction for evaluating the job of proclaiming the authentic *logos* of Christ to the authentic contemporary *ethos* of his Church, with authentic Christian *pathos*.

Preaching will continue to be a vital part of authentic Christian Spiritual formation. In the postmodern context, preaching will need to involve the whole Community. It will inspire the congregation towards Active faith. It must be given in a context that engages one's full Sensual experience. It will need to display Humility. It will involve the congregation through Inquiry. It will be Irreverent towards institutional modernism. It will address real and Relevant issues. It will be held up as a Necessary task of the authentic Christian leader, and the content will always be the properly exegeted true Text of the Scriptures.

Some Recommendations

The next chapter will examine each of these critical issues for the Spiritual formation of postmoderns through exposure to the Word of God. I will use examples from my own postmodern congregation, The Place, to illustrate and recommend ways of placing attention on these nine critical issues in an actual emergent church setting. These nine important themes, Community, Activity, Sensuality, Humility, Inquiry, Irreverence, Relevancy, Necessity, and Text, can guide us in being the authentic Church of Jesus Christ in this new postmodern paradigm. Put in a different order we can spell the acronym C-H-R-I-S-T-I-A-N to help us memorize and apply these nine important themes of true Christian preaching in the postmodern context so that, with authentic *pathos*, we might better proclaim the true *logos* of God's Word to the contemporary *ethos* of today's contemporary, Western churches through **C**ommunity, **H**umility, **R**elevancy, **I**nquiry, **S**ensuality, **T**ext, **I**rreverence, **A**ctivity, and **N**ecessity.

Chapter 5

Putting it All Together:
The Logos, Ethos and Pathos of Spiritual Formation

Community

"In a Christian community, everything depends on whether each individual is an indispensable link in a chain."[208]

Dietrich Bonhoeffer

For Spiritual formation through preaching to be both authentically Christian and authentically postmodern, it will need to involve the whole community in its expression, from the early stages of exegesis to its final public verbal presentation. It cannot be a solo act by a professional expert who closets himself away with books until the moment he ascends the pulpit platform. The postmodern preacher must engage his community. He must exegete his community. He must truly know, love, and serve his community by inviting them along on a journey of listening to the revealed Word of God together.

There are many ways to involve one's community in the early stages of exegesis. At our church, this is attempted by inviting the community to join in on a weekly meeting around the identified

---

208   Dietrich Bonhoeffer, Life Together (New York, NY: Harper and Row, 1976), 90.

text for that week. This is a planning meeting for the upcoming Sunday service. Usually present are the preacher, the music worship leader, the administrator, a visual artist, the prayer leader, and any other interested members. This often includes ministry leaders such as youth leaders, children's workers, small-group leaders, and church elders.

The preacher comes with his homework done. The hard work of textual exegesis has been done on his own. He has examined the text in all its contexts (original language, culture, history, genre, text, and theme). He has consulted commentaries. He brings all of his homework to the group and they wrestle with the text together. Often the music worship leader has also done some homework and examined the themes of the text for responsive engagement with the Word in song. The prayer leader or visual artist may also have been engaging the text during the week and have each brought their own interpretations.

The group, representing the larger community, listens to the text together and asks, "What does this mean? What did it mean to the original hearers, and what does that mean for us?" There may be disagreements. There will be different points of view. What surfaces is a rich tapestry of living believers listening to God's Word together. Their combined insights inform the continued development of what will take place at the Sunday service. There is seriousness to the actual exegesis of the text. The group does not equally weigh careful exegesis with personal opinion. This group is not about pooling ignorance. However, the preacher is not the only one listening to the text and preparing his message in private. The group helps one another engage the Word and discern its message.

At our church, we also have a team of Bible teachers, rather than just one main preacher. This team must work together to present unified teaching. At the same time, there is an inherent diversity in the group. Diversity is highly valued among postmoderns. The team model can communicate and demonstrate the unity and diversity of the Christian body. During the week, the congregation is encouraged to study and reflect on the passage, in small groups or individually. This is a communal approach to the whole process of listening to

God's Word, from the early stages of exegesis to the delivery of a Sunday sermon.

One of the things this approach to communal exegesis does is combat certain modernist cults. The contemporary Christian leader battles several modernist cults. There is the "cult of the expert." If someone has written a book or is on television, wears a lab coat, or is even merely from out of town, he is considered an expert. With the rejection of modernist rationalism, postmoderns have not rejected the modernist awe of experts, but have merely adopted a pattern of believing their own choice of experts, habitually failing to examine their claims for falsehoods. With the community gathering around the texts of Scripture together, the group can challenge preconceived or misplaced trust in the teaching of experts, which on careful examination of actual texts may prove to be erroneous.

Another modernist cult is the "cult of celebrity." The local pastor can never compete with the popular entertainment icons or the Christian celebrities who dominate the public media and private imagination. Like in the "cult of the expert," people will simply give attention and allegiance to celebrities. Every public servant is compared to the most popular celebrity. The preacher is compared to Chuck Swindoll. The worship band is compared to U2. But the real hero ought to be the local guy who works hard, every week, to serve his congregation by helping them pay attention to real texts and real lives. It is easy to entertain, especially from a distance or in short bursts.

Entertainment is an addiction for contemporary culture; many churches compromise their integrity to keep their people amused. Some churches are like Broadway, while others are more like Barnum and Bailey. With ever more elaborate and expensive technology and techniques, Western churches attempt to compete with the dazzle of popular celebrity entertainment. Jacque Ellul has pointed out that technology is like a Trojan horse in the city of God.[209]

Whether it is a show or a circus, it is not a community. The shift to postmodernism has shown us that the real work of Christian

---

209   See Jacque Ellul, The Technological Society (New York, NY: Vintage Books, Random House, 1964).

pastoring is to be a real, known person who leads a real, known community in life and faith. The weekly gathering of representatives of the real, known community combats the "cult of celebrity." It anchors the journey of faith to reality. An authentic postmodern pastor is able to publicly say to his community, "Cut me some slack," because he is a member of the community, not an expert or a celebrity. The ministry of a pastor is not a performance, but a sharing in the journey of life and faith. His task is to help create Christ-centered community.

Another modernist cult that a communal approach to listening to the Word of God combats is the "cult of individualism." Individualism and all its consequences are in direct opposition to the interest of God's Holy Spirit in building the united body of Christ. The rugged, self-reliant individual of American lore and the polite, private individual of Canadian society are modernist enemies to the Christ-centered community. The postmodern preacher must model the kind of relationally interdependent, life-on-life communal enmeshment that will help the Word of God be attended to in this new era.

The actual public presentation of the Bible teaching must also model the communal aspect of authentic postmodern Christianity. The message cannot be a lecture. There can be no invisible wall between the speaker and the congregation. It must be a conversation. Sometimes there must literally be interaction between speaker and listener. It must be done in a natural, friendly, relational way.

At our church, we may begin with a question related to the theme of the passage of Scripture we are listening to that week. The question gets the congregation interacting relationally. The speaker may then engage in answering the question himself. This bridges the preacher into the dialogue. Likewise, throughout the message there may be interaction through questions, invitations to reflect on a subject, the sharing of a humorous anecdote, an interview with someone, or even just a conversational tone.

The tone of the message is set by the attitude of the speaker. If one believes that this is a lecture or performance, one will project that kind of formal, divisive atmosphere. If one assumes that this is a group of friends who have gathered to listen to the Word of God together, one will project a casual atmosphere of friendly, warm, mutual respect and familiarity that invites others into the faith community on a journey in communal conversation. For preaching to be both authentically Christian and authentically postmodern, it will need to cultivate a sense of community.

Humility

*"I used to think, that God's gifts were on shelves one above
another and the taller we grew, the easier we can reach
them. Now I find, that God's gifts are on shelves one beneath
the other and the lower we stoop, the more we get."*

F. B. Meyer[210]

For Spiritual formation through preaching to be both authentically Christian and authentically postmodern, it will need to display honest humility. The shame of the human race is that people take themselves far too seriously, while not taking God seriously enough. The greatest expression of humility in postmodern preaching is humor. Humor does not necessarily mean funny, but the Latin base of that word, *humus*, meaning "earth" or "soil." The most basic meaning of being human is that people are from the earth. Humans are humble, "earthy" creatures. And one of the most basic human experiences is to laugh (and cry), especially at one's self.

The authentic postmodern Christian preacher will use humor, not to entertain, but to engage his audience. Self-deprecating humor is one of the surest ways to connect to the *pathos* of the postmodern congregation. The common experiences of life are earthy and humorous. As one humbly shares one's life and faith journey, one earns a hearing from a generation that is looking for authenticity and integrity. Modernist preachers found a hearing through formality and seriousness. Postmoderns are looking for commonality, humility, and *humus*.

This is the humble, joyful, life-affirming engagement of humor. C. S. Lewis understood this when he had his demonic character, Screwtape, divide humor into four categories: "Joy, Fun, the Joke Proper, and Flippancy."[211] The first two are of no use to the demons,

---

210   As quoted by Paul Lee Tan in the Encyclopedia of 7,700 Illustrations: Signs of the Times (Rockville, MD: Assurance Publishers, 1984), 572.
211   C. S. Lewis, The Screwtape Letters (New York, NY: Simon & Schuster, 1961), 49.

Screwtape says, because joy and fun, like music, are actually the stuff of heaven and unintelligible to demons. Lewis also quotes Martin Luther, saying, "The best way to drive out the devil, if he will not yield to texts of Scripture, is to jeer and flout him, for he cannot bear scorn."[212] "Satan," said Chesterton, "fell through force of gravity. We must picture Hell as a state where everyone is perpetually concerned about his own dignity and advancement, where everyone has a grievance, and where everyone lives the deadly serious passions of envy, self-importance, and resentment."[213]

The Scriptures, which the Church preaches, are themselves full of the *humus* of life. The encounters between God and humanity are often humorous stories simply because, like a good joke, they are full of juxtaposition and shock. To truly understand the message of Jesus' parables, one must encounter the funny shock of the story: a camel going through the eye of a needle, a man building his house on sand, a rich man running to meet his wayward son. Jesus, what a joke! But then the punch line and wham! The story of God's grace, understood for the ridiculous shock that it is.

There will always be a surprise because one is always dealing with a strange being (the God of the Universe) encountering strangers (real, *humorous* people). The divine comedy is about a stranger who is completely other (Holy), courting his unholy creatures. It is the juxtaposition and shock of the unexpected that catches one off guard. It grabs one's attention and has one reacting with laughter and awe. Shocked into laughter and then silenced into awe, one recognizes one's true self and the true God himself. This humble realization is a true appropriation of revelation. God initiates with his revelation, and his creatures respond with realization or ignorance.

The postmodern revolution can teach the Church to communicate the humility of the proper approach to listening to God's Word, as well as the humble content of that Word. The authentic postmodern Christian preacher will utilize the *pathos* of humble, *humus*, human humor in her proclamation of the Scriptures.

---

212   Martin Luther, cited by C.S. Lewis, The Screwtape Letters, 5.
213   C. S. Lewis, Introduction to The Screwtape Letters, ix.

Relevance

"Being a relevant Christian is about four words:
Love God. Love people"

Kary Oberbrunner[214]

Spiritual formation through preaching must address relevant issues of people's real lives. David Buttrick said of preachers, "We must engage in a kind of rediscovery of actual lived experience so that homiletic images are in touch with how God may impinge upon inter-human awareness."[215] Relevant does not mean relative. The message of Christian preaching is not relative to the whims of contemporary culture. And preachers do not *make* it relevant. It is intrinsically relevant to this or any culture whether individuals recognize it or not. Relevant means "prophetic" in the sense that God's Word must be addressed to the relevant issues of this contemporary age and in the relevant language, culture, and history of this age. One must prophetically relate God's revealed truth to one's contemporary existential reality.

Recently, a friend complained that on the Sunday following the September 11 terrorist attacks in the United States, his pastor preached a sermon without once mentioning those events. It was probably the thing that most occupied people's minds that morning, yet his sermon did not relate to it at all. To be relevant is to be aware of and involved with what our community is aware of and involved with. Like the men of Issachar, all preachers need to be men who "understood the times and knew what [God's community] should do" (1 Chron. 12:32 NIV).

This is not about merely using scenes from *The Simpsons* to demonstrate that one is "hip" to today's trends. One may use *The*

---

214   Kary Oberbrunner, a young pastor of student ministries in a church outside Columbus, OH. This is also the basic point of Oberbrunner's new book, The Journey Towards Relevance: Simple Steps for Transforming Your World (Lake Mary, FL: Relevant Books, 2004).

215   David Buttrick, Preaching the New and the Now (Louisville, KY: Westminster John Knox Press, 1998), 138.

Simpsons, current events, or other items from popular culture to relate the eternal *Word* to this present cultural experience. The distinction is that one will use anything from popular imagination to help one understand the *logos* of the Scriptures. One does not start with the message of *The Simpsons* and look for a Bible verse to illustrate one's point. One begins with the Word of God and looks for any way to relate its message to the real lives of one's congregation.

Christian preachers must know the language, culture, and history of their communities to help people listen to the Word of God in their context. Christian leaders live in two worlds: God's revealed reality and their own existential realities. It is the former that must define the Church and be the measure of the latter. This has always been the case for the biblical community. Eugene Peterson writes, "God does not put us in charge of forming our personal spiritualities; we grow in accordance with the revealed Word planted in us by the Spirit."[216]

When the people of God were in exile, they wondered, "How can we sing the songs of the Lord while we are in a foreign land?" (Ps. 137:4 NIV). The emergent Church finds itself in a foreign land today. Alan Roxburgh argues that the Church is in "exile" and must recover its soul, a passion in mission.[217] One might ask, what does this look like? It will essentially look the same as in every era: the people of God gathering together to listen to the Word of God read, sung, prayed, and preached in the relevant context of their day and place.

The Hebrew faith community adjusted to its new Babylonian context. They were without land, a temple, or a king. They listened to God's Word in small groups, in new settings at synagogues, and responded with the new language of apocalyptic poetry. Through each stage in God's salvation history, the people of God have begun with the *Word*, and then they have applied what has been revealed to their existential experience, in a garden, in a new promised land, in a kingdom with a temple, and in captivity without a temple. The

---

216   Eugene Peterson, Eat This Book: The Holy Community at Table with Holy Scripture (Vancouver, BC: Regent College Publishing, 2000), 9.

217   See Alan Roxburgh, Reaching a New Generation: Strategies for Tomorrow's Church (Downers Grove, IL: InterVarsity Press, 1993).

people of God have experienced many settings, yet have always been the people of the *Word*, relating its revealed message to their ever-changing contemporary cultural reality.

At our church, we read, sing, pray, and preach through whole books of the Bible over weeks or months. We listened to the whole of God's story in Genesis over eight months. We engaged God's message, but related it to the contemporary lives of our community as the Word was reflected on and applied. In December, we recognized the season of Advent, but did not stop listening to Genesis. Genesis was our anchor to God's world. Advent bridged us into our world. Some of the leaders thought we should stop our study in Genesis for the Advent time, especially for our Christmas service. "It's got nothing to do with Christmas!" someone argued. But it was counter-argued that it has everything to do with Christmas. The whole of the Scriptures is the story of Christmas. We stayed with the text throughout the season, and a rich juxtaposition provided some deeper insights relevant to both God's Word and our world. Jesus is on every page, as is God's Word for our contemporary experience.

Likewise, while teaching a youth Sunday school class, one leader wanted to ask the youth to suggest which topics they wanted to cover during the school year. I suggested that we ought to simply read through the Gospel of Mark, letting these topics surface out of the text. This was attempted, and everyone was surprised that all the subjects were covered, but in context of God's greater story, rather than using the Scriptures as proof text for our topical list. This is what Dick Lucas and John Stott and the other founders of "Proclamation Trust" urge preachers to do. We ought to faithfully and relevantly teach God's message in the Bible texts. Once, at a Dick Lucas preaching seminar, an Anglican priest exclaimed, "But that makes it so easy! I don't have to come up with snazzy new topics to preach on all the time! I can just teach the text!"

Jason Van Bemmel asks,

> So, who wants to be relevant? Well, I do. I want to speak the truth of God in a way that my generation will understand. But I don't think we'll do that by

capturing the White House or the music charts. I think we'll only do that by loving one another and the world around us radically and sacrificially—just like Jesus.[218]

Finally, to be real and relevant in this generation is to be relational. Faith Worship Center in Greensville, SC, uses this statement on their website: "real, relevant, relational … that's faith!"[219] Someone once said, "This generation doesn't care if it's true. They want to know if it's real." To be real means it works relationally, in everyday, lived-out relationships. The postmodern preacher must be a relational communicator, building community. And, speaking humbly, he must also proclaim the relational message of the Scriptures.

---

218   Jason Van Bemmel is a seminary student and freelance writer who works for New Covenant Christian School in Bel Air, MD.

219   See http://www.fwcag.com/

Inquiry

"It is the mark of our true and holy religion that it courts inquiry and denies no species of fair investigation."

Bishop Daniel Wilson[220]

Spiritual formation through preaching to postmoderns will need to engage congregation through inquiring questions. Someone once pointed out that Jesus asked questions and told stories, while many in churches today give answers and tell lectures. The mantra of sixties Western rebels was to "question all authority." They are now the grandparents of the emergent Church generation. It is simply a part of the fabric of life and faith that one challenges all authority and questions every proposition. On average, this generation is also highly educated and well informed of local and global events, and trends and ideas.

Therefore, preaching to postmoderns can never simply be dogmatic assertions of propositional statements about biblical content or a preacher's pet topics. Rather, the postmodern Christian preacher must engage people with his own real questions, and listen to and incorporate his audience's own questions into any interaction with Christian texts and ideas. One must encourage the kind of habit the Bereans were commended for in Acts, as they "examined the Scriptures every day to see if what Paul said was true" (Acts 17:11b NIV). The preacher must be the humble representative of God's Word who invites the community into a relevant dialogue, asking questions about what God says and wants, and representing the quandaries of his people.

It is a part of the very essence of the record of God's Word that it holds up to fierce inquiry. The Bible record gives names, dates, and locations for its "salvation history" events. Christianity is not a faith based on people's personal experiences or opinions, but the record of a communicative God who has revealed his character and will through real events. These events are attested to as historical facts.

---

220   As quoted by Jay Gurrnet at The Place, April 24, 2005.

This is not human fantasy, but divine revelation, and he expects his people to know, love, and serve him correctly.

Of course, there are essential doctrines of the faith that must be believed for one to be a Christian "believer." There is specific content to the Christian faith. But one's understanding of these essential beliefs, as well as one's ongoing reception of God's continuing revelation through his written Word, must be personally appropriated. Faith is not a matter of people blindly agreeing to rote information. Our questioning, searching, doubting, and inquiring are all vital to the authentic Christian life and faith development, especially in this postmodern context.

At our church, we attempt to encourage inquiry through many avenues. Sermons often begin with a query. The congregation is invited to dialogue about a question related to the theme of that week's section of Scripture. Also, people are invited to meet the preacher after the service at our own café for questions, arguments, or concerns about the message. Small groups are encouraged, to allow for diversity in opinions or practices. Our website provides space for people to share their questions and ideas. Doug Pagitt invites his congregation to participate in a sermon development discussion on Tuesday nights and then even encourages what he calls "progressional dialogue" wherein anyone can interject a comment, question, or challenge as a vital part of the Sunday sermon.[221]

We are interested in everyone's opinion on anything. However, the question that must guide all discussions is always, what does God say about it? The dictum "In essentials unity; in nonessentials disunity and charity over all" is a good one. Certainly there is disagreement about what is "essential." But we agree that the essentials are revealed in God's Word, and it is there that we must debate, question, study, and examine to see if what anyone teaches or believes is true.

---

221   Pagitt, Preaching Re-Imagined. 107

Sensuality

"God created us as multisensory creatures and chose to reveal himself to us through all of our senses. Therefore, it's only natural that we worship him using all of our senses."

Dan Kimball[222]

Spiritual formation through preaching to postmoderns must be given in a context that engages one's full sensual experience. With the rejection of modernist rationalism, a greater awareness of the sensorial experience of life and worship is emerging. This is seen in the importance of music, mystery, and beauty in emergent churches. Postmoderns are not interested in anything that is perceived as merely intellectual. The appropriately irreverent, relevantly real, grounded, Christ-centered faith community will engage the whole person in worship.

This is not a new thing for the faith community. The aberration was the modernist practice of intellectualizing and sanitizing the worship experience. The Old Testament experience of worship, at the Sinai Tabernacle or the Jerusalem Temple, was a fully sensorial experience. Imagine a gathering of the masses bringing their daily sacrifices. There were the sounds of the prayers of thousands of human voices mixed with the chants of hundreds of priests, and the cries of thousands of animals mixed with the blasting of worship instruments. There were the sights of the throngs, the blood, the candles, the altar, the smoke, the dazzling gold, and the colorful priestly garments; the smells of the incense, the burnt grain and meat, and the blood, feces, and sweat. There were the feelings of the crowd on one's body, the washing water on one's face and hands, the altar fire on one's skin, the smoke in one's lungs, the blood-soaked ground between one's toes, and the animal, vibrantly alive and then limply dead in one's hands. There were the tastes of the dryness of the mouth in prayer, the tears of joy and repentance, the flavors of

222   Dan Kimball, The Emerging Church: Vintage Christianity for New Generations (Grand Rapids, MI: Zondervan, 2003), 128.

the sacrifices, and the feasting on food before and after. This was an intensely sensual experience.

In Revelation, John re-imagines this kind of sensual experience when he describes worship in the heavenly realms. There are trumpets and voices, rainbows and lightning, blood and incense, rumblings and tears, and sweet and sour scrolls. In the premodern Western Church, there was a greater sensual experience than what grew out of the modernist enlightenment. European cathedrals were designed to enhance the appreciation of God through all five senses. These attentions to the sensual experience in worship must be regained in the postmodern Church to help this emerging generation attend to God.

At our church, we are attempting to experiment with sights, sounds, touches, tastes, and smells. We use "PowerPoint," not only to project song lyrics, but also to show beautiful images throughout the worship experience. We listen to songs, speeches, and silences. We are highly touch-oriented (relational). We feel and smell the bodies around us in worship, and we feel and taste the bread and wine, and the coffee and desserts afterwards. The Christian life is a five-sense, corporeal experience. It is rooted in the *humus* of our bodies in time and space. It is realized through our physical beings. And the authentically Christian, postmodern preacher will engage her congregation's fully sensual lives.

Text

*"That's biblical preaching. That's what we're trying to
do; taking a text, living in that text, inviting other people
into that text, and allowing the text to speak its Word to
us as unencumbered as possible by our distortions."*

Daryl Johnson[223]

The content of authentic Spiritual formation through preaching in
the postmodern setting must continue to be the properly exegeted
true text of the Christian Holy Scriptures. John Stott wrote,

> Here, then, is the preacher's authority. It depends
> on the closeness of his adherence to the text he is
> handling, that is, on the accuracy with which he has
> understood it and on the forcefulness with which
> it has spoken to his own soul. In the ideal sermon
> it is the Word itself which speaks, or rather God in
> and through His Word. The less the preacher comes
> between the Word and its hearers, the better. What
> really feeds the household is the food which the
> householder supplies, not the steward who dispenses
> it. The Christian preacher is best satisfied when his
> person is eclipsed by the light which shines from
> the Scripture and when his voice is drowned by the
> Voice of God.[224]

The great Old Testament preacher Ezra "devoted himself to the
study and observance of the Law of the LORD, and to teaching its
decrees and laws in Israel" (Ezra 7:10 NIV). He found himself leading
the people of God during a time of transition into a new orientation.

223   President of Regent College, Daryl Johnson, during a public lecture at Regent
College, Vancouver, BC, Feb. 2005.
224   John Stott, The Preacher's Portrait: Some New Testament Word Studies (Grand
Rapids, MI: William B. Eerdmans Publishing Company, 1961), 30.

Yet he relied on what the leaders of the faith community had always done: leading the people in listening to the texts of God's Word in their contemporary setting. He exegeted the Word to understand its *logos* content. He conveyed the Word in the *pathos* of living practice. He taught the Word in the context of his contemporary *ethos*.

There is a description of Ezra's method in Nehemiah 8. He stood before the assembled people, opened the Word, and he (and other Levites) read it and interpreted it so that the people could understand it. The people responded in prayer, praise, weeping, and worship. They started with the text, applied it to their lives, and responded to it with faith. They did not begin with some topics that they thought their people needed to learn about and then find some proof texts to teach mere "traditions of men." Rather, they let God speak through his revealing Word. Ezra simply read the text "from daybreak till noon" (Neh. 8:3 NIV) before he and the other priests instructed. Many evangelical churches today do not have even a short reading of the text as a part of their service outside of the sermon.

Jesus argued in his great "Sermon on the Mount" that until heaven and earth disappear, not even an *iota* or a *keraia* will vanish from the Scriptures. And those who *luse* (loosen or destroy) any bit of it "will be least in the kingdom of heaven, but whoever practices and teaches [it] will be called great in the kingdom of heaven" (Matt. 5:19 NIV). Unfortunately, in some churches, the Word of God is not only adhered to loosely, it is twisted to mean whatever people want it to mean. One could argue that contemporary Christianity is a combination of legalism and spiritualism wrapped up in Christian clichés.

The greatest emphasis must be placed on the postmodern preacher's job of doing careful exegesis, faithful practice, and proper instruction of biblical texts. This is what Paul was commending Timothy to do when he said, "What you heard from me, keep as the pattern of sound teaching, with faith and love in Christ Jesus. Guard the good deposit that was entrusted to you—guard it with the help of the Holy Spirit who lives in us" (2 Tim. 1:13-14 NIV). Training in the study, practice, and teaching of the Word is crucial for Christian leadership in every age, but especially in this postmodern era when texts and rational communication are deconstructed and dismissed as relative.

There is another enemy of proper Christian attention to the study, practice, and teaching of texts today: a uniquely postmodern erroneous belief in an antithesis between "head knowledge" and "spiritual knowledge." This myth assumes that "spiritual" wisdom is something that drops out of the clear blue sky directly from God, rather than being something revealed by God to human minds and hearts. This is a great contributing evil to some of the chaos in our contemporary scene. Sincere, well-meaning men and women, chiefly because of an ignorance of basic biblical truths, teach heresy in the name of Christ. If proper exegesis of biblical texts is ignored, ignorance will be studied, practiced, and taught.

At our church, we are endeavoring to study, practice, and teach the Word of God together. The teachers are committed to faithfully exegeting the actual texts of the Scriptures. As previously mentioned, we teach through whole books of the Bible. We invite our congregation to test everything that is taught against their own understanding of the texts through personal study. The members of the team of teachers also hold one another accountable to be faithful representatives of the Word. We help one another, ask one another, commend one another, and forgive one another when we fail. The authentically Christian, postmodern preacher must be committed to being a serious student of the Word first, and then to being one who exposes the actual texts of God's revelation to her congregation.

Irreverence

"Irreverence is the champion of liberty and its only sure defense."

Mark Twain[225]

Authentic Spiritual formation through preaching to postmoderns will necessarily involve irreverence towards anything that is merely modern or institutional. In practice, this may shock some who confuse merely institutional or modern things with sacred things. Mark Twain also apparently said, "Sacred cows make the best hamburger."[226] In rejecting the religions of modernism, postmoderns may seem irreligious. This is certainly how Jesus was viewed as he challenged what he called "the traditions of men" (Mark 7:8 NIV), which were the "sacred cows" of his day.

With the death of European Christendom, and as the age of modernism disappears, preaching can no longer assume a common belief in or language of "the traditions of men." When John McLeod Campbell preached his excellent sermon "What Does It Mean to Be a Christian?" he could say, "if the end of our being be to know and enjoy God..."[227] rightly assuming that his audience had a familiarity with the *Westminster Catechism*. This cannot be assumed today. People must be made familiar with the wonderful theology of the *Westminster Catechism*, but it cannot be assumed that they have even ever heard of it, let alone that they are familiar with its excellent contents. This generation is more familiar with *The Simpsons, Survivor, American Idol,* and the content of a *Beatles'* song.

When Paul called the pagan Athenians "very religious" (Acts 17:22 NIV), he was being irreligious. He was disregarding "the traditions of men" of his day and speaking their language. In the modernist age, one could assume that most people in Western culture were churched. In this age, one must assume the opposite. In a modernist church, one can assume that the people want to be there;

225   As quoted on thinkexist.com, http://en.thinkexist.com/quotations/irreverence/
226   Ibid.
227   Michael Jinkins, John McLeod Campbell (Edinburgh, UK: St. Andrews Press), 43.

they respect the pastor because he is a pastor, and they understand the language and traditions. At The Place, we try to assume that they do not necessarily want to be there, they don't know anything, they don't like or respect us, and they are not interested in what we have to say. Then we try to plan what we must do to win them over and introduce them to the God who reveals himself in Christ in the Scriptures. This may seem irreverent, but we call it "missional."

Another aspect of irreverence is the language, culture, and history of this age. There is a new *ethos* of basic societal norms and mores that do not relate to some of the modernist "traditions of men." Some things that are commonly considered properly "Christian" in one generation are not reverenced as good, or even "Christian," in the next. It is ironic that a modernist will want the "truly Christian traditional hymns" properly sung in his church, while Queen Elizabeth I apparently forbade some of these same hymns in churches because she condemned them as vulgar "Geneva jigs." This is also true of speech, dress, attitudes, and habits.

Author Jacob Chanowski is quoted as saying, "It is important that students bring a certain ragamuffin, barefoot, irreverence to their studies; they are not here to worship what is known, but to question it."[228] Often faith is misplaced in what Christians assume to "know." There is a need to question what is "known" to determine if it is actually what God reveals to be true for life and faith practice, or merely "the traditions of [the] men" of the last generation.

There is a postmodern casualness that is appropriate for the language, culture, and history of this age. This is reflected in casual speech, dress, attitudes, and habits. Again, these things may shock some who are more accustomed to a modernist *ethos*, but what is important is to differentiate between what is truly of God, which must always be reverenced, and what is merely a "tradition of men," which may be reverenced by one generation, but not another. The authentically Christian postmodern preacher will discern the difference and preach with appropriate irreverence.

---

228   As quoted on http://quinnell.us/natural/quotes.html

Activity

"Leadership in the church community is unfaithful to the Spirit if this intimacy is not fostered in Word, sacrament, and action for justice."

Dietrich Bonhoeffer[229]

Authentic Spiritual formation through preaching in the postmodern ear will inspire the congregation towards active faith. Haddon Robinson writes, "The preacher that can use the imagination to paint a compelling and tangible picture of a preferred future for the listener, will lead the people toward a more meaningful experience."[230] Postmoderns are critical of anything that is merely theoretical. They want to see how it really works in practice. They are more concerned about how it works in practice than how, or even if, it works in theory.

The Christian leader must help his flock put their faith into practice. People of this generation can be enamored with heroes from any religion, race, moral creed, or political persuasion if they are perceived as "making a difference in the world." They can be (rightly) passionate about ecology, human rights, or justice issues. Unfortunately, faith is so privatized; it is not popularly seen as being something that actively engages real life. Preaching must engage the congregation members' passions and real lives, and make plain how faith must be practiced in the real world.

Seeing faith put into action will take time. But regular exposure to the Word of God will bring the changes in people's hearts and habits. The Desert Father Abba Poemen taught, "The nature of water is soft, that of stone is hard; but if a bottle is hung above a stone, allowing the water to fall drop by drop, it wears away the stone. So it is with the Word of God; it is soft and our heart is hard, but the man who hears the Word of God often, opens his heart to the fear of

---

229   Dietrich Bonhoeffer, quoted in Geffrey B. Kelly and F. Burton Nelson, The Cost of Moral Leadership: The Spirituality of Dietrich Bonhoeffer (Grand Rapids, MI: William B. Eerdmans Publishing Company, 2002), 58.
230   Haddon Robinson, Imagine the Difference: Motivating a Change in the Listener's Experience. http://www.preaching.org/difference.html.

God."[231] Relevant, inquiring, textually-based preaching of the Word of God will wear away at emergent people to motivate them to grow in worship and work in the Kingdom.

We are experimenting with this at our church. After we studied the book of Acts together, a group began to organize what has come to be called "Place Acts." It is a database of people and their talents, interests, and resources. It has been communicated that everyone who is a part of our community ought to be on the list, and the list is updated through periodic surveys and an active website. Church leaders manage this database. When a need arises, people who have a connecting interest are contacted. From helping a member move to commissioning ministry leaders, "Place Acts" has helped us put faith into action. The postmodern preacher must help his congregation put faith into action.

---

231   Abba Poemen, The Sayings of the Desert Fathers, quoted in Christianity Today Magazine (vol. 45. no. 13, Oct. 22, 2001), 40.

Necessity

"In this connection we must observe that, though preaching is necessary for the whole of creation, it is particularly useful to men."

Humbert of Romans[232]

In genuine postmodern Christian faith, Spiritual formation through preaching will be held up as a necessary part of any authentic and healthy church of Jesus Christ. David Buttrick stated, "Speaking is our primary task."[233] Douglas John Hall said, "Ministers are recalled to the teaching office."[234] John Stott laid out five theological arguments that "leave us without excuse" in being convinced "of the indispensable necessity" of preaching for today.[235] These five arguments come from the five biblical doctrines of God, Scripture, the Church, the pastorate, and the nature of preaching.[236] The Apostles gave their "attention to prayer and the ministry of the word" (Acts 6:4 NIV), and Paul instructed Timothy to devote himself "to the public reading of Scripture, to preaching and to teaching" (1 Tim. 4:13 NIV). Somehow, in many circles, preaching has come to be considered optional.

At our church, we are attempting to communicate and demonstrate the necessity of preaching. From the beginning, there have been people who would like to drop the weekly verbal proclamation from the program. But our leadership is convinced of the necessity of preaching for the health and legitimacy of our church. We plan a menu of teaching for the coming year. We balance Old and New Testament, narrative and prophecy, epistle, topics, and issues. We incorporate the seasons of the Church, the nation, and

---

232   Humbert, writing in the thirteenth century, from Early Dominicans: Selected Writings (Mahwah, NJ: Paulist Press, 1982), 201.

233   Buttrick, 106.

234   Douglas John Hall, The End of Christendom and the Future of Christianity (Harrisburg, PA: Trinity Press, 1997), 49.

235   John Stott, Between Two Worlds: The Art of Preaching in the Twentieth Century (Grand Rapids, MI: William B. Eerdmans Publishing Company, 1982), 92–93.

236   Ibid, 93.

the year. We honor local and global events. However, we never stop listening to the text of God's Word read and taught in context.

Biblical preaching is an essential means of shaping Christian spiritual formation. The public reading and interpreting of God's recorded revelation exposes his people to the very *pneuma* (breath) of the living God. Nothing else can claim this: not singing, praying, working, nor giving. These things are all the responses to his Spirit breathing life into his people. It is through his Word exposed to his people that they are convicted, converted, and commanded. Preaching may look and sound different in this postmodern age, but it will remain necessary for the life of the Church as it has done in every age of God's salvation history.

The essence of authentic Christian preaching can be seen throughout the panorama of the entire story of God's redemptive history, recorded in the Scriptures. The fundamental task of the spiritual leader has always and only been to listen to God's Word, understand God's meaning, and proclaim it to his contemporary community. The Christian leader is to lead his people to pay attention to God. In these last days, God is paid attention to through the text of his spoken Word, the Bible (Heb. 1:1–3). The primary call of the Christian leader, then, is to continue to exegete the texts of God's Word and teach it to his community.

How could any Christian person "hate" that, sleep through it, or cheer for its absence during a Christian gathering? Either God's Word is being talked about, but not truly preached and understood, or the message is being understood, but it is not really God's Word. Neither scenario is what God expects of authentic preaching in his gathered covenant community. As John Stott points out, it is when the Church has neglected to execute its first duty to authentic, exegetically-based, expository preaching that it has experienced its eras of decline and weakness in strength, numbers, and vitality.[237]

237 Stott writes, "it is clear … that God hinged the welfare of his people on their listening to his voice, believing his promises and obeying his commands." He then quotes Edwin C. Dargan (A History of Preaching, Vol. 1, A.D. 70–1572, Grand Rapids, MI, Baker Book House, 1968), "Decline of Spiritual life and activity in the churches is commonly accompanied by a lifeless, formal, unfruitful preaching" (Between Two Worlds, 114).

Authentic Christian preaching ought never be long, boring, rationalistic lectures that are propositional, authoritarian, and opinionated in nature. It does not necessarily mean three-point, deductive, dogmatic sermons. It will always be prophetic messages that exegete God's revealed text and expose the people of God to the Word of God. This is what expository preaching is: exposing God's people to God's Word. This is the "baby" that ought to be kept. The "bathwater" that ought to be tossed out will be any style that does not communicate the meaning of God's Word, or any well-communicated message that is not God's Word. People must take the text very seriously and take themselves less seriously.

As the "bathwater" of modernist Christianity flows down the drain of history, the "baby" of authentic Christian belief and practice must be saved and cradled in new forms for a new generation. These nine important themes—Community, Humility, Inquiry, Sensuality, Text, Irreverence, Activity, and Text—can guide us in listening to and proclaiming the authentic Word of God in this new postmodern paradigm. These themes will also help us test the Bible teaching we receive, to determine if it reaches the goal of being high *logos*, high *ethos*, and high *pathos*. This is the true high calling of both those who proclaim and those who receive spiritual formation through that proclamation. As St. Paul wrote, "Test everything. Hold on to the good" (1 Thess. 5:2).

Appendix A
The Survey

Survey Questions

Your Name: _____

The Name of Your Church: _____

A - Tell me about your church:

1. On average, how many people attend your main church service?

    __ 30–99 __ 100–149 __ 150–499 __ 501–1000 __ 1001+

2. What is the average age of the majority group in your church?

    __ 10–15 __ 16–20 __ 21–25 __ 26–30 __ 31–35 __ 35–40

3. For how many years has your church been meeting?

    __ 1–5 yrs. __ 6–10 yrs. __ 11–15 yrs. __ 16–20 yrs. __ 20+ yrs.

4. How much time do the following elements take up in your average service?

    Music / Singing _____ min.   Announcements _____ min.

    Preaching _____ min.   Prayer _____ min.

    Scripture Reading _____ min.

    Other (_____) _____ min.

5. What (if any) changes would you like to see in your church over the next five years?

_____

_____

_____

_____

_____

B - Tell me about yourself:

1. How old are you?

___ 20–25 ___ 26–30 ___ 31–35 ___ 35–40 ___ 40+

2. For how many years have you been in full-time ministry?

___ 1–5 ___ 6–10 ___ 11–15 ___ 16–20 ___ 20+

3. What best describes your current level of education?

___ secondary school   ___ post-secondary diploma

___ some graduate school   ___ graduate degree

___ M.Div.   ___ seminary training

___ post grad. degree

4. What would you say are your leadership gifts?

_____

_____

5. What life events, ministry experiences, or people have been your greatest ministry influences?

_____

_____

C - Tell me about your preaching:

1. What have you been preaching over the last 12–18 months?

_____

_____

_____

_____

2. Why have you been preaching these things?

_____

_____

3. What (if any) preaching plans do you have for the next 3–18 months?

_____

_____

_____

4. Why are these your preaching plans?

_____

_____

5. How would you define "biblical teaching"?

_____

_____

6. Describe your typical sermon preparation.

_____

_____

_____

_____

7. How many hours do you spend preparing a typical sermon?

__ 1–5 __ 6–10 __ 11–15 __ 16–20 __ 20+

Appendix B
The Follow-Up Interview Questions

The following is the list of follow-up interview questions for the ten representative emergent church leaders chosen from all the survey respondents.

Survey Follow-Up Interview Questions

1. What formative experiences in your life have most influenced your approach to preaching and communicating God's Truth?

2. When I asked you how you would define "biblical preaching," you said

"_____." What did you mean by "_____"?

3. Can you tell me more about that?

4. When I asked you to describe your typical sermon preparation, you said

"_____." What did you mean by "_____"?

5. Can you tell me more about that?

6. What specific exegetical tools do you personally use to interpret biblical texts?

7. Do you believe expository preaching is relevant to the emerging church?

8. Why?

9. Where do you see evidence of "expository preaching" being abandoned or continued in the emerging church?

10. What would you say is the most important task of a leader in the emerging church?

Appendix C
The Statistical Analysis

Statistics for Ten Respondent Churches

Respondent Church Affiliations:

Baptist (4)   Brethren (1)   Lutheran (3)
Independent (1)   Vineyard (1)

Respondent Church Nationalities Represented:

New Zealand (4)   United States (3)
Canada (2)   England (1)

Average Size of Respondent Churches: 190

Average Age of Respondent Church Members: 21.5

Average Number of Years Respondent Churches have been
Meeting: 7.5

Average Minutes Spent During Church Services for:

Music / Singing: 19.8   Prayer: 7.6

Announcements: 5.7   Scripture Reading: 5.9

Preaching: 21.8   Other: 15.5

Average Age of Respondents: 35.7

Respondents' Average Years in Full Time Ministry: 10.3

Average Level of Education Among Respondents: graduate degree

Leadership Gifts Listed by Respondents:

communication (4)	inspiration	leadership
mentoring	implementing	vision (3)
direction	evangelism	prophesy
passion	empowering	music
thinking	catechism	training (2)
worship	discernment	creativity
hospitality teaching (2)	pastoral care	writing
entrepreneur	courage	preaching (2)
motivating	imagination	planning
min. to poor encouragement (3)		

Average Hours Respondents Spend in Sermon Preparation: 9.7

Bibliography

Adams, Peter. "The Preacher and the Sufficient Word." When God's Voice is Heard. Downers Grove, IL: Intervarsity Press, 1995.

Allan, Ronald J. As the Worldviews Turn: Six Key Issues for Preaching in a Postmodern Ethos. *Encounter* Magazine, Winter 1996.

Allan, Tom. Is Our Preaching Out of Touch? *Faithworks* Magazine, July 2004.

Anderson, Walt. The Truth About the Truth: De-Confusing and Re-Constructing Truth, A New Consciousness Reader. New York, NY: G.P. Putnam's Sons, 1995.

Barna, George. Generation Next: What You Need to Know About Today's Youth. Ventura, CA: Regal Books, 1995.

Barnett, Paul. The Lost Art of Preaching. Vancouver, BA: Regent College course, 1999.

Bibby, Reginald W. Fragmented Gods: The Poverty and Potential of Religion in Canada. Toronto, ON: Irwin, 1987.

Bibby, Reginald W. Restless Churches: How Canada's Churches Can Contribute to the Emerging Religious Renaissance. Kelowna, BC: Wood Lake Books, 2005.

Blackby: Henry and Richard. Experiencing God. Nashville, TN: Broadman & Holman, 1998.

Blackby, Henry and Richard. Spiritual Leadership. Nashville, TN: Broadman & Holman, 2001.

Bockmuehl, Klaus. Listening to the God Who Speaks: Reflections on God's Guidance from Scripture and the Lives of God's People. Colorado Springs, CO: Helmers & Howard Publishers, 1990.

Bonhoeffer, Dietrich. Life Together. New York, NY: Harper and Row, 1976.

Borgmann, Albert. Crossing the Postmodern Divide. Chicago, IL: University of Chicago Press, 1992.

Bosch David, J. Transforming Mission: Paradigm Shifts in Theology of Mission. American Society of Missiology Series, No. 16. Maryknoll, NY: Orbis Books, 1993.

Burgess, R.G. (Ed.). Field Research: A Source Book and Field Manual. London: Allen & Unwin, 1982.

Brueggemann, Walter. Finally Comes the Poet. Minneapolis, MN: Fortress Press, 1989.

Butrick, David. Homiletic. Philadelphia, PA: Fortress Press, 1987.

Buttrick, David. Preaching the New and the Now. Louisville, KY: Westminster John Knox Press, 1998.

Buttrick, David. Speaking Between the Times: Homiletics in a Postmodern World in Theology and the Interhuman (Ed. Robert R. Williams). Valley Forge, PA: Trinity Press, 1995.

Carrell, Lori. The Great American Sermon Survey. Wheaton, IL: Mainstay Church Resources. 2000.

Carroll, Colleen. The New Faithful: Why Young Adults are Embracing Christian Orthodoxy. Plano, TX: Layola Press, 2002.

Carson, D.A. Becoming Conversant with the Emergent Church. Grand Rapids, MI: Zondervan, 2005.

Chapel, Bryan. Christ-Centered Preaching: Redeeming the Expository Sermon. Grand Rapids, MI: Baker Books, 1994.

Clapp, Rodney. A Peculiar People: The Church as Culture in a Post-Christian Society. Downers Grove, IL: InterVarsity Press, 1996.

Clements, Roy. Expository Preaching in a Post Modern World. Cambridge Papers, vol. 7, number 3, September 1998.

Copenhaver, Martin B., Anthony B. Robinson, and William H. Willimon. Good News in Exile: Three Pastors Offer a Hopeful Vision for the Church. Grand Rapids, MI: William B. Eerdmans, 1999.

Cowan, Thomas. Unpublished Doctoral Thesis, 1997.

Dargan, Edwin C. A History of Preaching: Vol. 1 From the Apostolic Fathers to the great Reformers A.D. 70 – 1572. Grand Rapids, MI: Baker Book House, 1968.

Dawn, Marva. A Royal "Waste" Of Time: The Splendor of Worshiping God and Being Church for the World. Grand Rapids, MI: William B. Eerdmans Publishing Company, 1999.

Dawn, Marva. Reaching Out Without Dumbing Down: A Theology of Worship for the Turn-of-the-Century Culture. Grand Rapids, MI: William B. Eerdmans Publishing Company, 1995

Dexter, L.A. Elite and Specialized Interviewing. Evanston, IL: Northwestern University Press, 1970.

Donovan, Vincent J. Christianity Rediscovered. Maryknoll, NY: Orbis Books, 2003.

Dumbrell, William J. The Search for Order. Grand Rapids: Baker Books, 1994.

Ellul, Jacque. The Technological Society. New York, NY: Random House, 1964.

Eslinger, Richard. A New Hearing. Nashville, TN: Abingdon Press, 1987.

Fee, Gordon and Stewart, Douglas. How to Read the Bible For All It's Worth. Grand Rapids, MI: Zondervan, 1982.

Flory, Richard W. and Miller, Donald E. Gen X Religion. New York, NY: Routledge, 2000.

Fowler, James W. Faith Development and Pastoral Care. Philadelphia, PA: Fortress Press, 1986.

Frost, Michael and Hirsch, Alan. The Shaping of Things to Come: Innovation and Mission for the 21st Century Church. Peabody, MA: Hendrickson Publishers, 2003.

Frew, Donald H. Pagans in Interfaith Dialogue: New Faiths, New Challenges. CoGWeb: http://cog.org/pwr/don.html

Frost, Michael and Alan Hirsch. The Shaping of Things to Come: Innovation and Mission for the 21st Century Church. Peabody, MA: Hendrickson Publishers, 2003.

Gibbs, Eddie. Church Next: Quantum Changes in Christian Ministry. Leicester: Inter-Varsity, 2000.

Gibson, Scott M. and Willhite, Kieth (Eds.). The Big Idea of Biblical Preaching: Connecting the Bible to People. Grand Rapids, MI: Baker Books, 1998.

Glaser, B.G. and Stauss, A.L. The Discovery of Grounded Theory. Chicago, IL: Aldine Press, 1967.

Green, Garrett. Imagining God: Theology and the Religious Imagination. San Francisco, CA: Harper and Row, 1989.

Grenz, Stanley and John R. Franke. Beyond Foundationalism: Shaping Theology in a Postmodern Context. 1st ed. Louisville, KY: Westminster John Knox Press, 2001.

Grenz Stanley, J. Theology for the Community of God. Carlisle: Paternoster, 1994.

Grenz, Stanley J., What Christians Really Believe - and Why. (1st ed.) Louisville, KY: Westminster John Knox Press, 1998.

Griffen, Em. The Mind Changers. Wheaton, IL: Tyndale House Publishers, 1976.

Guder Darrell, L., and Lois Barrett. Missional Church : A Vision for the Sending of the Church in North. Grand Rapids, Mich.: W.B. Eerdmans Pub, 1998.

Hahn, Todd and Verhaagen, David. Reckless Hope. Grand Rapids, MI: Baker Books, 1996.

Hall, Douglas J. The End of Christendom and the Future of Christianity. Pennsylvania, PA: Trinity Press, 1995.

Harris, R. Laird, Gleason L. Archer Jr., and Waltke, Bruce K. Theological Wordbook of the Old Testament. Chicago, IL: Moody Press, 1980.

Harvey, Barry. Another City: An Ecclesiological Primer for a Post-Christian World Christian Mission and Modern Culture. Harrisburg, PA: Trinity Press International, 1999.

Hebblethwaite, Brian. The Incarnation: Collected Essays in Christology. Cambridge: University of Cambridge Press, 1987.

Hesselgrave, David J. and Rommen, Edward. Contextualization: Meanings, Methods and Models. Grand Rapids, MI: Baker Book House, 1989.

Henderson, David. Culture Shift: Communicating God's Truth in a Changing World. Grand Rapids, MI: Baker Book House, 1999.

Hendrickson, William. More Than Conquerors (2nd. Ed.). Grand Rapids, MI: Baker Books, 1940.

Hilborn, David. Picking up the Pieces. Nashville, TN: Hodder and Stoughton, 1997.

Houston, James. "Making Disciples, Not Just Converts: Evangelism without Discipleship Dispenses Cheap Grace" (editorial). *Christianity Today* Magazine, October 25, 1999.

Hybels, Bill, Briscoe, Stuart and Robinson, Haddon. Mastering Contemporary Preaching. Portland, OR: Multnomah Press, 1989.

Jinkins, Michael. John McLeod Campbell. Edinburgh: St. Andrews Press, 1993.

Johnson, Alan F. The Expositor's Bible Commentary. Vol. 12. Revelation. Grand Rapids, MI: Zondervan, 1981.

Katz, L. "The Experience of Personal Change." (Ph.D. dissertation) Cincinnati, OH: Union Graduate School, Union Institute, 1987.

Keil and Delitzch: Commentary on the Old Testament, volume 9. Grand Rapids, MI: William B. Eerdmans, 1981.

Kelly, Geffrey B. and Nelson, F. Burton. The Cost of Moral Leadership: The Spirituality of Dietrich Bonhoeffer. Grand Rapids, MI: William B. Eerdmans Publishing Company, 2002.

Kennedy, George A. On Rhetoric. New York, NY: Oxford University Press, 1991.

Kimball, Dan. The Emerging Church. Grand Rapids, MI: Zondervan, 2003.

Lascalzo, Craig A. Apologizing For God: Apologetic Preaching To A Post Modern World. Review and Expositor, 93, 1996.

Lathrop, Gordon W. Holy People: A Liturgical Ecclesiology. Minneapolis, MN: Fortress Press, 1999.

LeCompte, M.D. and Preissle, J. Ethnography and Qualitative Design in Educational Research (2nd. Ed.). Orlando, FL: Academic Press, 1993.

Lewis, C. S. The Screwtape Letters. New York, NY: Simon & Schuster, 1961.

Lewis, Ralph and Lewis, Gregg. Inductive Preaching. Wheaton, IL: Crossway Books, 1983.

Lloyd-Jones, D. M. Preaching and Preachers. Nashville, TN: Hodder & Stoughton, 1971.

Marshall, C. and Rossman, G.B. Designing Qualitative Research. Thousand Oaks, CA: SAGE Publications, 1989.

McGrath, Alaster. Rattling the Cages. Vancouver, BC: Regent College course, 1994.

McGrath, Alister. The Unknown God. Grand Rapids, MI: Zondervan, 1999.

McGrath, Alister. Christian Theology: An Introduction. Oxford: Blackwell Publishers, 1994.

McLaren, Brian. "They Say It's Just a Phase." Next-Wave website, 2000. http://www.next-wave.org/Nove00/phase.htm

McLaren, Brian. A Generous Orthodoxy. Grand Rapids, MI: Youth Specialties Books, Zondervan, 2004.

McLaren, Brian. The Church on the Other Side: Doing Ministry in the Postmodern Matrix. Grand Rapids, MI: Zondervan, 2000.

McLaren, Brian. A New Kind of Christian: A Tale of Two Friends on a Spiritual Journey. San Fransisco, CA: Jossy-Bass, 2001.

McLaren, Brian D. and Anthony Campolo. Adventures in Missing the Point: How the Culture-Controlled Church Neutered the Gospel. El Cajon, CA: Emergent YS, 2003.

McLaren, Brian D. and Leadership Network (Dallas, TX). The Story We Find Ourselves In: Further Adventures of a New Kind of Christian. (1st ed.) San Francisco, CA: Jossy-Bass, 2003.

McLuhan, Marshall, Eric McLuhan, and Frank Zingrone. Essential McLuhan. London: Routledge, 1997.

McGrath, Alister, E. Christian Theology: An Introduction. Oxford: Blackwell Publishers, 1994.

Merriam, S.B. Qualitative Research and Case Study Applications in Education. San Francisco, CA: Jossy-Bass Publishers, 1998.

Mustard Seed Associates. "Does the Future Have a Church?" Conference, 2003. http://www.msainfo.org/date.asp?schedule=58&MainID=265

Myers, Ched. Reading the Bible in the New Millennium. *Sojourners* Online Magazine, http://www.faithandvalues.com/tx/00/00/03/30/3044/index.html

Myers, Joseph. The Search to Belong: Rethinking Intimacy, Community, and Small Groups. Grand Rapids, MI: Zondervan, 2003.

Newbigin, Lesslie. Foolishness to the Greeks. Grand Rapids, MI: William B. Eerdmans Publishing Company, 1986.

Newbigin, Lesslie. The Gospel in a Pluralist Society. SPCK, 1989.

Newbigin, Lesslie. Proper Confidence: Faith, Doubt, and Certainty in Christian Discipleship. Grand Rapids, MI: William B. Eerdmans Publishing Company, 1995.

Nicholls, Bruce J. Theological Education and Evangelization: Let the Earth Hear His Voice (Ed. J.D.Douglas). Minneapolis, MN: World Wide, 1975.

Niebuhr, H. Richard. The Meaning of Revelation. New York, NY: Macmillan Publishing Company, 1960. 111.

Oberbrunner, Kary. The Journey Towards Relevance: Simple Steps for Transforming Your World. Lake Mary, FL: Relevant Books, 2004.

Ockenga, Harold J. "Proclamation For a New Age," Toward a Theology for the Future (Pinnock, Clark and Wells, David, Eds.). Carol Stream, IL: Creation House, 1971.

Pagitt, Doug. Preaching Re-Imagined: The Role of the Sermon in Communities of Faith. Grand Rapids, MI: Zondervan, 2005.

Palmer, Earl. The Enormous Exception: A Commentary on the Sermon on the Mount Waco, TX: Word Books Publishers, 1986.

Patton, M.Q., Qualitative Evaluation Methods (2nd. Ed.) Thousand Oaks, CA: SAGE Publishers, 1990.

Peterson, Eugene. Christ Plays in Ten Thousand Places. Winnipeg, MB: CMBC Publications, 1999.

Peterson, Eugene. Eat This Book: The Holy Community at Table with Holy Scripture. Vancouver, BC: Regent College Publishing, 2000.

Peterson, Eugene. Leap Over A Wall: Earthy Spirituality for Everyday Christians. San Francisco, CA: HarperCollins, 1997.

Peterson, Eugene. Reversed Thunder. San Francisco, CA: HarperCollins, 1988.

Popcorn, Faith. The Popcorn Report. New York, NY: Doubleday Books, 1991.

Postman, Neil. Amusing Ourselves to Death: Public Discourse in the Age of Show Business. New York, NY: Penguin Books, 1984.

Resner, Andre Jr. Preacher and Cross: Person and Message in Theology and Rhetoric. Grand Rapids, MI: William B. Eerdmans Publishing Company, 1999.

Rhee, Jong Sung. "A New Anthropology from the Perspective of Theology." Theology in the Service of the Church: Essays in Honor of Thomas W. Gillespie. Wallace M. Alston (Ed.). Grand Rapids, MI: William B. Eerdmans Publishing Company, 2000.

Riddell, Michael and Knowledge Society for Promoting Christian. Threshold of the Future: Reforming the Church in the Post-Christian. London: SPCK, 1998.

Roberts, Wes and Glenn Marshall. Reclaiming God's Original Intent for the Church. Colorado Springs, CO: NavPress, 2004.

Robinson, Haddon. Biblical Preaching: The Development and Delivery of Expository Sermons. Grand Rapids, MI: Baker Books, 2001.

Robinson, Haddon. Imagine the Difference: Motivating a Change in the Listener's Experience. http://www.preaching.org/difference.html

Robinson, Haddon. Expository Preaching in a Narrative World. Michael Duduit Interview: *Preaching* Magazine. July/August 2001.

Roxburgh, Alan J. Reaching a New Generation : Strategies for Tomorrow's Church. Downers Grove, IL: InterVarsity Press, 1993.

Roxburgh, Alan, J. The Missionary Congregation, Leadership, and Liminality Christian Mission and Modern Culture. Valley Forge, PA: Trinity Press International, 1997.

Sangster, W. E. The Craft of the Sermon. London: The Epworth Press, 1954.

Sherman, R.R. and Webb, R.B. "Qualitative Research in Education: A Focus" in R.R. Sherman and R.B. Webb (Eds.), Qualitative Research in Education: Focus and Methods. Bristol: Falmer Press. 1988.

Stake, R.E. "Case Studies" in N.K. Denzin and Y.S. Lincoln (Eds.) Handbook of Qualitative Research. Thousand Oaks, CA: SAGE Publishing, 1994.

Stott, W. "A Note on the Word *kuriake* in Rev. 1:10." *NTS* 12, 1965.

Sine, Tom and Christine. http://www.msainfo.org.

Smith, Chuck. The End of the World - As We Know It: Clear Direction for Bold and Innovative Ministry in a Postmodern World. 1st ed. Colorado Springs, CO: WaterBrook Press, 2001.

Snyder, Howard A. and Daniel V. Runyon. Decoding the Church: Mapping the DNA of Christ's Body. Grand Rapids, MI: Baker Books, 2002.

Spong, John Shelby. Rescuing the Bible from Fundamentalism: A Bishop Rethinks the Meaning of Scripture. New York, NY: HarperCollins Publishers, 1991.

Spong, John Shelby. The Sins of Scripture: Exposing the Bible's Texts of Hate to Reveal the God of Love. New York, NY: HarperCollins Publishers, 2005.

Stackhouse, John Jr. Speaking in Tongues: Crux, Vol. 25, No. 4. Vancouver, BC: Regent College, 1999.

Staniforth, Maxwell (translator). Early Christian Writings. London: Penguin Books, 1988.

Steiner, George. No Passion Spent. New Haven, CT: Yale University Press, 1996.

Stetzer, Ed. Planting Churches in a Postmodern Age. Nashville, TN: Broadman & Holman, 2003.

Stott, John R.W. Between Two Worlds: The Challenge of Preaching Today. Grand Rapids, MI: William B. Eerdmans Publishing Company, 1982.

Stott, John R.W. I Believe in Preaching. London: Hodder & Stoughton, 1982.

Stott, John R.W. The Preacher's Portrait: Some New Testament Word Studies. Grand Rapids, MI: William B. Eerdmans Publishing Company, 1961.

Sweet, Leonard. Aqua Church. Grand Rapids, MI: Zondervan, 1999.

Sweet, Leonard. Carpe Manana. Grand Rapids, MI: Zondervan, 2001.

Sweet, Leonard. Post-Modern Pilgrims: First Century Passion for the 21st Century World. Nashville, TN: Broadman & Holman, 2000.

Sweet, Leonard. Postmodern Pilgrims. Nashville, TN: Broadman & Holman, 2000.

Sweet, Leonard. Soul Salsa. Grand Rapids, MI: Zondervan, 2000.

Sweet, Leonard I. and Andy Crouch. The Church in Emerging Culture: Five Perspectives. El Cajon: EmergentYS, 2003.

Sweet, Leonard I., Brian D. McLaren, and Jerry Haselmayer. "A" Is for Abductive: The Language of the Emerging Church. Grand Rapids, MI: Zondervan, 2003.

Taylor, S.J. and Bogdan, R. Introduction to Qualitative Research Methods. New York: Wiley Publishers, 1984.

Tomlinson, Dave. The Post-Evangelical. London: Triangle, 1995.

Tompson, Mark D. A Clear and Present Word: The Clarity of Scripture. Downers Grove: Inter-Varsity Press, 2006.

Tuck, William P. Toward a Theology of the Proclaimed Word. Review and Expositor, Winter, 1984.

Tugwell, Simon. Early Dominicans: Selected Writings (The Classics of Western Spirituality). Mahwah: Paulist Press, 1982.

Volf, Miroslav. After Our Likeness: The Church as the Image of the Trinity Sacra Doctrina. Grand Rapids, MI: William B. Eerdmans, 1998.

Ward, Pete. Mass Culture: Eucharist and Mission in a Post-Modern World. Oxford: Bible Reading Fellowship, 1999.

Ward, Pete. Liquid Church. Carlisle, Cumbria Peabody, MA: Paternoster Press, Hendrickson Publishers, 2002.

Webber, Robert. Ancient-Future Evangelism: Making Your Church a Faith-Forming Community. Grand Rapids, MI: Baker Books, 2003.

Webber, Robert. The Younger Evangelicals: Facing the Challenges of the New World. Grand Rapids, MI: Baker Books, 2002.

Wilcock, Michael. The Message of Revelation: I Saw Heaven Open. Leicester: Intervarsity Press, 1989.

Wilkinson, Lorne. "The Bewitching Charms of Neopaganism." *Christianity Today* Magazine, September 27, 2001.

Willhite, Keith and Gibson, Scott M. (Eds.). The Big Idea of Biblical Preaching: Connecting the Bible to People. Grand Rapids, MI: Baker Books, 1998.

Wilson, Jonathan R. Living Faithfully in a Fragmented World: Lessons for the Church from Macintyre's After Virtue. Harrisburg, PA: Trinity Press International, 1997.

Wood, D. R., Packer, J.I., Marshall, I. Howard, Millard, A.R., Wiseman, D.J., Wood, D.R. (Eds.). New Bible Dictionary. Leicester: Intervarsity Press (3rd Ed.), 1996.

Woodhouse, John. The Preacher and the Living Word. Leicester: Intervarsity Press, 1995.

Yaconelli, Mike. Stories of Emergence: Moving from Absolute to Authentic. Grand Rapids, MI: Emergent YS, Zondervan, 2003.

Yancey, Philip. Reaching for the Invisible God. Grand Rapids, MI: Zondervan, 2000.

VITA

The author of this work is James Andrew Prette. Born April 13, 1962, in Victoria, BC, he lived in Victoria for his first 23 years. During that time, he completed high school and then a bachelor of Fine Arts degree at the University of Victoria, majoring in visual arts and theatre. After a brief career teaching middle school art and drama, he joined the staff of Young Life of Canada, moving to Kelowna, BC. After five years, he moved to Vancouver, BC, to lead Young Life in the Greater Vancouver Region. There he completed a Master of Divinity at Regent College. In 1996, he moved back to Victoria to lead Young Life on Vancouver Island. Shortly after this time he completed the D.Min. program at Gordon-Conwell Theological Seminary. James continues to live in Victoria, BC, with his wife, Liz, and their three children. He is the Greater Victoria regional director, and the director of staff education and training for Young Life of Canada. He is also a Teaching Pastor at Lambrick Park Church.